A BRIEF HISTORY OF PORTUGAL

BLAZING THE TRAIL OF A VOYAGE-SHAPED NATION

DOMINIC HAYNES

CONTENTS

HOW TO GET A FREE SURPRISE HISTORY EBOOK

Get access to the surprise history ebook below and free and unlimited access to all my future books by joining my community.

Scan with your camera to join

INTRODUCTION

Burrowed within the Iberian Peninsula, to the west of Spain, lies Portugal, an established member of the European Union whose name derives from the Roman word for the town Portus Cale. The 35,560 square mile country is one of the founding members of NATO and contributed significantly to the formation of the euro currency. Yet, it remains inconspicuous and often overlooked among the countries on the southwest rim of the continent.

Its history is littered with visionaries and leaders who made it possible for humanity to undertake some of its most extraordinary adventures—the Discoveries. Owing to the impetus of many of its leaders, Portuguese caravels traveled across seas, using some of the best practical and scientific knowledge of the time. They navigated the Far East, Africa, and the South American continent. They amassed wealth, conquered territories, and brought unprecedented new items and ideas to Europe.

This book highlights Portugal's enigmatic and global history, describing the quirks that make it unique and tracing the trails it blazed on its eventful path to where it is today. Claiming one of the oldest fixed borders, Portugal provides a patchwork of various beautiful landscapes. The Portuguese have a seductive and easy-going lifestyle that descends from their rich history, particularly evident in their love for food. Their contemporary life also reveals a penchant for individu-alism and anarchy, adding a unique twist to their cultural fabric.

As we peel back the layers of Portugal's complex and multifaceted identity, it's essential to journey back to its very roots. Before the Discoveries that heralded Portugal's age of exploration, before the formation of NATO, even before the Romans set foot on the Iberian Peninsula, the land that would become Portugal was home to prehistoric communities whose legacies are etched in stone and soil. As you turn the page, we'll traverse these ancient landscapes, meeting the early hunters and gatherers who first called this land home, setting the stage for millennia of cultural evolution, conflict, and global influence. Let's embark on this historical voyage together, from the Paleolithic era to the modern day, to uncover the enduring spirit of Portugal.

1

PREHISTORIC PORTUGAL, THE ROMAN EMPIRE, AND THE INSTITUTION OF "ROMAN PEACE" (PREHISTORY–200 AD)

The beginnings of human life in present-day Portugal have been lost in the sands of time, but they likely trace back around 500,000 years. The earliest inhabitants were lower Paleolithic hunters and gatherers who used simple stone tools. These tools have been discovered in different sites, most concentrated in the central coastal region. History suggests that these hunters and gatherers had a lithic culture, meaning they relied heavily on stone tools for hunting, gathering, and crafting, a practice common in Western Europe at the time. This lithic culture is associated with *Homo erectus*, the modern human's predecessor.

Millennia later, nearly 100,000 years ago, as suggested by archeologists, the subspecies Neanderthal appeared in Portugal. Neanderthals are famed for their heavy muscular build and for living in small hunting groups. Their artifacts in Portugal lie in different sites. A Neanderthal tooth was found in a cave in Estremadura and is now considered the oldest hominin, or human relative, fossil discovered in the country. Modern humans, known as *homo sapiens*, are said to have arrived 35,000 years ago. They supplanted the Neanderthals completely and spread fast throughout the country. How and why that happened remains an intriguing question for historians and archeologists.

Were Neanderthals unable to compete, slowly succumbing over time? Or were they systematically and deliberately slaughtered? Did the subspecies mix, and were Neanderthals absorbed gradually into rival communities? Answers to these questions are generally left to speculation. A child's skeleton suspected to be 24,500 years old was discovered in Leiria in western Central Portugal. It is believed to form a morphological basis for a Neanderthal-modern human hybrid. In the Furninha cave, on the southern slope of the Peniche peninsula, other Neanderthal-type bones have been found, but scientists disagree on how far back they date.

What is agreed, though, is that around 5500 BC, during the Middle Stone Age, a distinct culture emerged in the lower Tagus Valley. This culture, originating from

Andalusia, was unique for several reasons. Beyond their architectural achievements, which included beehive-shaped huts, they were pioneers in the region's pottery, agriculture, and metalwork. Their pottery, often intricately decorated, suggests a society with both the time and the skill for artistic endeavors. The introduction of agriculture indicates a shift from nomadic hunting and gathering to a more settled lifestyle, and their early forays into metalwork show technological advancements. These elements together make a case for a complex and evolving society that played a crucial role in shaping the subsequent cultures of what would become modern-day Portugal.

The history of settlement in Portugal is a subject of lively debate among historians, especially concerning the timelines. One of the most well-supported historical records suggests that the Iberians were the first major group to significantly influence the Peninsula and arrived around 3000 BC. These early people are thought to have migrated from North Africa, and their arrival marked such a profound impact that the Peninsula was named Iberia after them. They were primarily agricultural and fishing communities, and they left behind an assortment of artifacts that give us glimpses into their lives.

Around 1000 BC, another significant group entered the scene: the Celtic tribes. Originating from Central Europe, the Celts crossed the Pyrenees mountains and moved westward, bringing with them their distinct language, art, and social structure. Over time, they established numerous hilltop settlements across the country. These Celtic communities proved resilient, continuing to exist even after the later Roman conquest.

By the 9th or 8th century BC, a new group, the Phoenicians, entered the complex tapestry of Iberian history. Hailing from the eastern Mediterranean, specifically from regions now part of modern-day Lebanon, Syria, and Israel, the Phoenicians were renowned seafarers and traders. Attracted by Iberia's wealth of resources, such as copper, silver, and iron, they embarked on maritime voyages to the region. Notably, they settled in places like Gadir (current-day Cádiz) and had a lasting impact by introducing writing techniques among other cultural exchanges.

By the 8th century BC, the geopolitical landscape was again shifting dramatically due to two emerging Mediterranean powers, Carthage and Rome. The Carthaginians, originally a Phoenician colony from modern-day Tunisia in North Africa, had by this time established a strong foothold in the southern parts of the Iberian Peninsula and built a significant military center at Murcia. They were well on their way to dominating the region, leading many to believe that the fate of modern-day Portugal and Spain would be as part of a Carthaginian Empire.

On the other hand, Rome was a rising city-state on the Italian Peninsula that had begun to extend its influence across the Mediterranean. Although Roman leaders were growing increasingly suspicious and watchful of Carthaginian activities, they took no decisive action at this point, effectively ceding power over the Iberian Peninsula to their soon-to-be archrivals. This early deference would set the stage for later conflicts and shifts in control that would define the region.

As if the Iberian Peninsula wasn't already a melting pot of cultures and influences, the 7th century BC saw yet another entrant: the Greeks. Originating from city-states along the Aegean Sea, Greek traders and colonists began arriving in Iberia, introducing agricultural innovations like olive cultivation and vineyards. They primarily traded in the region of Ampurias, Catalonia, adding another layer to the diverse cultural mosaic of ancient Iberia.

With the stage set for a dynamic intermingling of cultures, the 6th century BC witnessed a renewal of Phoenician involvement, specifically from the settlers in Gadir. In North Africa, they sought assistance from their Carthaginian brethren—also known as Punics—to fend off attacks from local tribes. The Carthaginians, or Punics, had their own interests in Iberia, naming it *Spania* or *Span*, which translates to "the land filled with rabbits." Initially, their focus was on exploiting and trading the abundant silver resources. However, over time, they expanded their agenda to include the enslavement of local tribes to build their military power, setting the stage for their confrontation with Rome in the First Punic War.

With the Mediterranean civilizations like the Phoenicians, Carthaginians, Greeks, and Romans marking their influence primarily along the coastal regions and southern parts of the Iberian Peninsula, one might think the interior remained untouched. However, that was far from the case. By the 5th century BC, the Celts had become dominant in the northern parts of modern-day Portugal and Spain. They spread quickly throughout the rest of the Peninsula, intermingling and ruling alongside the Iberians to create the Celtiberian culture.

Equally enigmatic are the Basques, primarily located in today's mountain regions of Spain and France. Their origins remain a topic of academic debate; some posit they could be remnants of the Celtiberians, while others believe they descend from earlier Stone Age inhabitants. Despite the uncertainty surrounding their origins, the Basques have managed to preserve some privileges of self-government over the centuries. Today, they continue to speak both their native language, Euskara, in addition to either French or Spanish.

With such a tapestry of influences stretching from the early millennia BC to the Roman era, the Iberian Peninsula has always been a dynamic and complex region. By the time we reach the 3rd and 2nd centuries BC, different civilizations had already left their marks in various ways, from the Phoenicians in the south to the Celts and Basques in the north. This perpetually shifting landscape was what Rome would later invest in, both to counter Carthaginian advances and to consolidate its own burgeoning empire. As a result of Rome's newfound commitment to the region, many of today's urban centers in Portugal and Spain have Roman origins. For instance, the Lisbon harbor, initially used by the Carthaginians, was expanded by the Romans and became a strategic administrative center for their province of Lusitania.

The First Punic War unfolded between 264 and 241 BC, serving as the opening act in a series of conflicts between Rome and Carthage. After their defeat, Carthage sought to rebuild its power by establishing a foothold in Spain under General Hamilcar Barca. His son-in-law, Hasdrubal, took over and founded a new capital, Cartagena, also known as New Carthage. Rome, increasingly concerned about Carthage's activities in Spain, struck a treaty with Hasdrubal. According to this treaty, Carthage agreed not to expand its influence north of the Ebro River and not to attack Saguntum, an independent town and an ally of Rome.

However, in 220 BC, the political landscape changed abruptly when Hasdrubal was assassinated. Hannibal, Hamilcar Barca's son, took command. In 219 BC, at 26 years of age, Hannibal defied the treaty by besieging and capturing Saguntum. This act of aggression, influenced by Carthage's previous losses and territorial reparations from the First Punic War, triggered the Second Punic War between 218 and 201 BC.

The Second Punic War was a tipping point for Roman involvement in the Iberian Peninsula. Until then, Rome had been relatively hands-off, but after defeating Carthage and assuming control over their territories, Rome decided to make a lasting presence in the region. Perhaps they were enticed by the area's rich agricultural and mineral resources and access to cheap labor.

After Hannibal captured the city of Saguntum, an ally of Rome, the Roman Senate demanded a Carthaginian withdrawal. Carthage's refusal led Rome to declare war, sparking the Second Punic War. Recognizing Rome's naval strength, Hannibal opted for a land-based invasion. He led his troops from Spain through Gaul and over the Alps to reach Italy's Po River plain in 218 BC. Despite losses endured during this arduous journey, his army remained formidable. Establishing a foothold in northern Italy, he then engaged Roman forces.

After winning several victories, including the pivotal Battle of Cannae in 216 BC, Hannibal advanced to Capua—then Italy's second-largest city—hoping to rally Italian states against Rome. Despite this, he held back from directly assaulting the Roman capital. Rome responded with a defensive strategy, employing various tactics under different generals. Quintus Fabius Maximus was known for his "delay and harass" approach. This stalemate continued until 211 BC when Rome recaptured Capua. In a crucial turn of events in 207 BC, Hasdrubal, Hannibal's brother, attempted to reinforce him for a united assault on Rome. Gaius Nero, commanding Rome's southern army, made a daring move north and defeated Hasdrubal at the Battle of the Metaurus, preventing the Carthaginian forces from uniting.

Hannibal maintained his position in southern Italy until 203 BC when the Carthaginian ruling council recalled him to Africa. The order came as Roman forces, now under the command of Scipio Africanus, threatened Carthage itself. Hannibal's departure marked the first time in over a decade that Italy was free of foreign troops. During this prolonged conflict, Sicily became Rome's primary source of food. At the same time, Rome's military pressure, led by General Publius Scipio, successfully expelled the Carthaginians from their strongholds in Spain between 215 BC and 210 BC.

After Scipio's victory, he set his sights on the Carthaginian homeland. Departing for Africa in 204 BC, he established a beachhead. Initially offered terms of surrender, the Carthaginian council changed their minds at the last minute, deciding to put their trust in one final battle. Hannibal led the Carthaginian army in this decisive conflict, which took place near Zama—located in present-day Tunisia. The Carthaginians were soundly defeated at Zama, leading them to accept Rome's terms for peace. As a result, Rome gained control over the Mediterranean islands.

In the period after the Second Punic War, Rome expanded its control over much of the southern and eastern Iberian Peninsula, encountering a variety of local tribes, including the Celts. One particular tribe, the Lusitani, resisted Roman influence. However, after the assassination of their leader, Viriathus, in 140 BC,

Roman military leader Decius Junius Brutus success-fully defeated them. In 25 BC, Caesar Augustus, the first Roman Emperor, designated Merida as the capital of the Roman province of Lusitania, which included areas now part of modern-day Portugal. Galicia was later established as its own province, governed in the 2nd century AD by a later Roman ruling family, the Antonines.

2

END OF ROMAN PEACE, THE VISIGOTHS AND THE MOORS (201 AD–1000 AD)

The period of Roman peace, known as Pax Romana, generally extended until around 180 AD. It was characterized by stable governance, flourishing trade, and infrastructural developments, including the production of honey, wine, and wheat. Roman road systems enhanced communication, such as the Via Augusta that connected Cádiz, a southern Spanish port city, to the Pyrenees mountain range. Latin became the administrative language, and large Roman cities were trade, culture, and government hubs. Residents of Hispania (Roman Spain) could achieve Roman citizenship upon meeting specific criteria. Hispania produced notable figures like Seneca, Martial, and Lucan in the 1st century and Hadrian in the 2nd century, while the 4th century saw the rise of

Theodosius the Great, born in Hispania. Christianity was officially adopted by the Roman Empire in the early 4th century, with regions like Hispania transitioning to the new faith over a period of time.

During the 3rd century AD, internal conflicts weakened Rome, leading to a decline in its power. Seeing an opportunity, the northern Germanic tribes, who had previously been kept at a distance, started advancing into Roman territory. By mid-century, the Visigoths had extended their influence into what is now known as Romania, specifically in the region then called Roman Transylvania, and they also began raiding Rome's eastern provinces.

This dynamic changed in the middle of the 4th century when the Asian Mongolian Huns pushed the Visigoths out of their territories. Fleeing the Huns, the Visigoths were permitted by Rome to cross the Danube River and settle in Roman lands. However, mistreatment by Roman officials led to disputes and uprisings, culminating in a Visigothic victory over Rome. The Visigoths then settled in what is now Bulgaria, and their forces were integrated into the Roman army.

By the late 4th and early 5th centuries, the Roman Empire was divided into western and eastern halves. Alaris the Visigoth made the Eastern Empire his puppet. He did not want to destroy Rome—he wanted to enslave it. He wanted to rule over his people, who had adopted Roman customs and embraced the Arian form of Christianity. Pursuing this aim, he attacked Italy and soon captured Rome itself. In response to these attacks from the eastern Goths, Roman military forces pulled back from other areas of the Italian Peninsula. Taking advantage of this withdrawal, other Germanic tribes moved in and took over territories in Portugal and Spain.

The Germanic invasion of the Iberian Peninsula started in 409, led by the Suebi, the Vandals, and the Alans. The Suebi settled in the north and the Vandals in the south, who then started moving toward Northern Africa. Meanwhile, the Visigoths encroached on southern Gaul from Italy. Under King Wallia (415–418), Emperor Honorius granted them land, and they set up a kingdom in Toulouse. In return, the king would clear Iberia of the Germanic tribes. He would later take back much of the Peninsula from the Suebi and rule for the rest of the 5th century.

In 507, the Visigoths were evicted by the Franks, another Germanic tribe. Their domain was reduced to the Iberian Peninsula, and they stayed there until 711. The three centuries when the Visigoths ruled were not peaceful. In addition to the troubles with the Germanic tribes who would eventually subjugate the Peninsula, civil wars were prevalent. In 554, General Belisarius led a campaign in the southern regions of Spain as part of the Byzantine Emperor's initiative to reclaim former Roman territories. Byzantium ruled the province and its capital in Córdoba, located in Southern Spain, until the Visigoths reconquered it in 616. During their rule, the Visigoths were a minority of the population. Already Romanized in part, they gradually adopted Roman habits and customs.

In 587, the Visigoth king removed all barriers to Romanization by converting to Roman Catholicism and renouncing Arian Christianity. The Visigoths adopted Latin, and in the 7th century, their laws and Roman laws were made into a single code. Despite their presence, the Visigoths never wholly integrated with the majority Roman population. They maintained a separate status, acting as a ruling class with their own elite social structure. In 710, a succession conflict arose among the Visigoths. One of the contenders sought assistance from the Moors, who were primarily inhabitants of Morocco. The term "Moors" originates from the Mauri, a community that is part of the Berbers, the indigenous peoples of North Africa.

At the beginning of the 8th century, Northern Africa was already under Arab conquest, and the Berbers had taken up Islam. Driven by religious zeal, Berber and

Arab armies, under the leadership of Berber Tariq, went through the Straits of Gibraltar into Spain. They defeated the Visigoths and swept aside the faction that had appealed to them. Most people were unhappy with their Visigoth rulers and remained sympathetic to the Moors. Within eight years, the Moors had conquered most of the Iberian Peninsula, except for the mountainous region of Asturias in the north. Explaining the rapid defeat of the Visigoths is challenging, as the most comprehensive accounts come from anecdotal Muslim sources written after the 10th century. The remnants of the Christian armies stayed in Asturias under a Visigoth noble, Pelayo. The city would become a pivotal center for the Reconquista, the nearly 800-year-long campaign led by Christian kingdoms to reclaim the Iberian Peninsula from Muslim Moorish rule.

After conquering the Peninsula, the Moors invaded France but were defeated by the Franks in 732. Nearly half a century later, Charlemagne, the Frankish emperor who had waged 53 campaigns across Western Europe to spread Christianity, invaded Spain. However, for the first time in his career, Charlemagne was compelled to retreat. Unable to capture Saragossa, he began his withdrawal. During this retreat, his forces suffered a devastating defeat at a mountain pass in the Pyrenees, an event later immortalized in the epic poem *Chanson de Roland*. The end of the century saw

Charlemagne return and take over Barcelona in 801. He arranged a defensive area around 100 miles south of France and called it the "Spanish March."

The Moors continued to dominate the Iberian Peninsula, except for a few Christian strongholds and the "Spanish March," until the end of the 11th century. During most of this period, the Umayyad dynasty ruled the region, a prominent Islamic family that had previously governed a vast empire stretching from Spain to India. Moorish domination was experienced the most in Andalusia. The Moors treated their Visigothic and Roman subjects with tolerance. They allowed Christian worship, and many Christian mercenaries enrolled in Muslim armies. Some Christians even rose high in the Moorish administration. It was common to see inter-marriages. The Moors introduced new crops like sugar, rice, figs, and dates, improving agriculture. They also introduced irrigation that Arab engineers would later extend. They expanded industries such as livestock farming, wool production, silk manufacturing, and mining.

During that period, trade prospered. Beautifully designed silk fabrics were exported in ships through the Mediterranean. The Moors also introduced an art renaissance and a revolution in literature and science at a time when many European countries were experiencing intellectual stagnation. The Arabs were leading the Western world. Through Arabic translations, the writings of ancient Greece found their way to the West. Translators were mostly Mozarab and Jewish scholars. Mozarabs descended from the pre-Muslim inhabitants who had kept their Christianity but adopted Arabic and Muslim customs. The knowledge transmission to the West would later accelerate, thanks to the Reconquista.

Córdoba quickly rose to be the leading intellectual center of Europe. It had a library of 400,000 books and a university visited by students from all over the world. People came there to study science, philosophy, and mathematics under Jewish, Christian, and Muslim professors. There was even an academy of music. There were many public baths and fountains. Houses had piped water supplies and balconies for the summer and hot air ducts under the floors for winter. The streets were stone-paved, and nearly every home had a garden.

Architecture also prospered, with the great mosque of Córdoba being built in 785 AD. It is one of the world's largest cathedrals, second only to St. Peter's Cathedral in Rome. The Alhambra Palace in Granada was built in the 13th century and is famous worldwide today. At its zenith, Moorish power was led by Caliph Abdur Rahman III (912–961) and Almansor (978–1002). In the northeast, the Moors conquered Barcelona in 985 and Santiago in 997. However, the Berbers, who were continuously reinforced from Africa, grew in power at the expense of the Moors. The death of Almansor led to internal conflicts that broke up the Moorish territories into smaller states, which in turn created an opportunity for the northern Christian kingdoms to advance their Reconquista efforts. During this period of disunity, Barcelona changed hands but was eventually retaken by the Moors, although their fragmented states prevented any further territorial gains.

The Arabs were one of the most sophisticated civilizations to inhabit Portugal. For five centuries, they infused their agricultural techniques and food practices into the cuisine of Hispania, making it one of the most diverse in Europe today. Many years of Arab occupation left Portugal with a culinary legacy rich in almonds, citrus fruit, and figs. Portugal and its neighboring nations became a food gateway that would conquer the West and influence modern food. Despite the visible culinary legacy, academic research on this topic is still in its early stages. Claudio Torres, a scholar and archaeologist of Arab descent, contends that a wealth of untapped historical documents can provide further evidence to support these culinary influences.

Most of what we know of this history today comes from records kept in Spain. Arabists specializing in gastronomy paint Portugal's identity nebulously, having been swept up by Arab culture. Another food researcher of Algarve cuisine says that Arab influence can still be seen all over the region regarding fruit. There may be no documented recipes, but you can tell that certain fruits were consumed because they were produced and sold. Historians refer to orchards with apricots and bitter oranges, for example.

As Chapter II comes to a close, we see that the Moorish rule over the Iberian Peninsula—replete with advances in architecture, governance, and even culinary practices —was a complex era marked by cooperation and conflict. However, the decline of Moorish power, particularly after the death of Almansor, set the stage for a new chapter in the history of the region: the Reconquista. The internal divisions among the Moors opened the door for the northern Christian kingdoms to regain lost territories and initiate a centuries-long campaign to recapture the peninsula. We will now delve into this pivotal period of the Reconquista, the rise of the Order of Aviz, and how these developments shaped the Portugal we know today.

3

THE RECONQUISTA, ORDER OF AVIZ, AND THE RISE OF PORTUGAL (1001–1580 AD)

In the 10th century, the northern Christian kingdoms were deeply divided, marked by internal conflicts and political intrigues. During this time, the first Christian kingdom, Asturias, founded by Pelayo—who initiated Christian resistance to Moorish rule—relocated its capital to Leon, situated in the northwest of modern-day Spain. Leon subsequently emerged as the leading Christian state. Adding to the internal strife was the County of Castile, a significant political entity in the central and northern part of the Iberian Peninsula. Opposing Leon's Visigothic traditions, Castile broke away to claim its independence. Despite these developments, the Reconquista, the campaign to reclaim territory from the Moors, made little headway. It wasn't until the 11th century that the Reconquista gained significant momentum. Throughout this tumultuous period, shifting alliances among Christian and Muslim states further complicated the effort to oust Moorish rule.

The Basque kingdom dramatically rose to prominence during the 10th century. At the same time, further to the east, the inhabitants of the Spanish March, under the leadership of Barcelona, secured their independence from the House of Charlemagne. As the 11th century dawned, a significant power shift occurred with the emergence of Sancho the Great. Sancho was the King of Navarre, a kingdom bordering modern-day Spain and France in the northern part of the Iberian Peninsula. He formed a strategic alliance with Castile, another prominent Christian state, to challenge and largely subdue Leon, the then-leading Christian power. The union was short-lived, and when Sancho died, Navarre was divided into Aragon and Navarre, two separate kingdoms. Castile's Ferdinand I completed the Leon conquest, so Castile became the nucleus of the Reconquista. He reclaimed the northern region of what is now Portugal from Moorish control and established it as a county, designating Coimbra, a city situated in central Portugal, as its capital. In 1085, Alfonso VI of Castile achieved a major milestone in the Reconquista by capturing Toledo.

After losing Toledo, the Moors asked a Berber dynasty, the Almoravids, for help. The Almoravids were Muslim fanatics led by Yussuf-ul-Tashvin, who had earlier defeated Alfonso of Castile, recovering most of what had been yielded to Islam. Alfonso resumed the struggle later on with the help of Rodrigo de Bivar, a nobleman otherwise called El Cid. El Cid was a self-seeking adventurer who had once served the ruler of Saragossa. However, he eventually transformed into a legendary Spanish hero. He seized control of Valencia and governed the city until he died in 1099 when it came under attack by the Almoravids.

Henry of Burgundy, a nobleman from the region of Burgundy in modern-day France, arrived in the Iberian Peninsula to contribute to the Reconquista, the Christian campaign against Moorish rule. His arrival and participation in the Reconquista were later than El Cid's and focused more on the Portuguese side of the struggle. The period of his appearance overlaps with the Crusades era, a series of religious wars in the Middle East aimed at reclaiming holy lands from Muslim rule. While the Reconquista and the Crusades were related but distinct movements, the fervor of the Crusades did influence Christian military efforts in the Iberian Peninsula.

Henry of Burgundy was rewarded for his contributions by being granted the County of Portugal and marrying Teresa of León, the daughter of Alfonso VI of León. His son, Afonso I of Portugal, commonly known as Afonso Henriques, took over the reins of authority at the age of 19 after the death of his father in 1112. Under the initial regency of his mother, Teresa, Afonso Henriques eventually led efforts to establish Portuguese independence from the Kingdom of León.

According to multiple historical accounts, Afonso Henriques led Portuguese forces to decisive victories against the Spaniards, which were instrumental in his recognition as the king of an independent Portugal in 1143. His dynasty would continue to rule Portugal until 1385. In 1139, the already renowned warrior initiated a series of campaigns against Moorish rule, capturing key strongholds and establishing the southern boundary of Portugal along the Tagus River. By 1147, German knights had already recaptured Lisbon from the Moors. Capitalizing on this success, Henriques and his army advanced up the Tagus River and secured Portuguese control over Lisbon.

While this happened, Catalonia and Aragon were united by marriage, forming a stronger Kingdom of Aragon, which now had access to the sea. During the mid-12th century, the progress of the Reconquista came to a halt and was even reversed due to another Berber invasion led by the Almohades. The Almohades were an even fiercer Muslim army descended from the Almoravids. Although they did not conquer all of Spain, they did manage to seize significant territories, pushing back the Christian forces led at that time by Alfonso VIII of Castile.

Under the guidance of the pope, Navarre, Aragon, and Castile finally combined forces and fought against the Almohades, winning the 1212 Battle of Las Navas de Tolosa. Ferdinand III of Castile and James I of Aragon would continue their victorious campaigns for fifty years. Ferdinand took Cádiz, Seville, and Córdoba, while James took the Balearic Isles and Valencia. They managed to expel the Almohades from Spain and Portugal, and soon after, during the 13th century, the whole Peninsula was led by Christians except Granada.

As could be expected, internal cooperation among the Christian kingdoms waned. With territories stretching to the Pyrenees, Navarre shifted its focus towards involvement in French affairs. Aragon concentrated on expanding its influence in the Mediterranean, while Castile focused on consolidating its newly acquired territories, albeit amid significant internal discord. In Granada, the Moors ruled for two more centuries. Alfonso XI of Castile successfully repelled the last

African invasion that supported the Moors in 1340. However, the Reconquista wasn't fully accomplished until 1492. That year, following the marriage of Isabella of Castile to Ferdinand of Aragon, the combined forces of their unified kingdoms captured Granada, the last Moorish stronghold.

In the two centuries leading up to the final expulsion of the Moors from Spain, Castile faced a series of governance challenges. These included periods of weak kingship and times of "royal minorities," which refer to instances when the throne was occupied by young, underage monarchs who lacked the authority to rein in the rising influence of the clergy and the aristocracy. Adding to Castile's internal strife were sporadic interventions from neighboring kingdoms like Navarre and Aragon, which took advantage of Castile's vulnerabilities to exert their influence or advance their interests. The 15th century, in particular, was marked by economic decline, political instability, and an increasing focus on orthodox Catholicism within Castile. In 1478, the Spanish Inquisition was established with the aim of eliminating heretical beliefs and practices within Spain. Then, in 1492, Jews, who had been tolerated until that point and had made significant contributions to Spain's cultural and economic development, were forcibly expelled from the country.

During this time, the Kings of Aragon were deeply involved in Italian affairs, marked by a complex web of dynastic marriages, warfare, and diplomatic maneuvers. Aragon acquired Sardinia and Sicily in the process. By the time it united with Castile, it was a strong power in the Mediterranean, with Barcelona as one of its leading ports. Meanwhile, Navarre was under French rulers. In 1512, after Aragon and Castile united, they went on to conquer Navarre and create the present-day boundaries of Spain and Portugal.

While the commonly accepted history of this period outlines specific sequences of events, an alternate account disputes the chronology but agrees on certain significant developments, like the union of Aragon and Castile. According to this secondary account, Afonso I of Portugal received charters to settle in the West. His son, Sancho I, governed the region between 1185 and 1211, and it was under his rule that various municipalities in central and eastern Portugal gained special privileges, attracting settlers from the north. Sancho even granted some Muslims these rights, although many others were enslaved. Sancho, aided by Crusaders, captured Algarve in 1189. Although he briefly lost control of the region in 1190, he reclaimed it in 1191, along with other territories south of the Tagus River. Upon Sancho's death, peace agreements were already in place, allowing his successor, Afonso II, to inherit a stable and peaceful kingdom. Afonso II focused on strengthening the power of the throne, even if it meant undermining the church.

In Portugal, Afonso II was not a warlike king. He repudiated the bequests of many estates to his brothers, focusing instead on internal governance. The pope recognized his sovereignty, although the specific timeline for this recognition was not mentioned. In the first year of his reign, Afonso II called a parliament meeting at Coimbra and summoned the prelates and nobility. This meeting resulted in significant concessions that strengthened the position of the church. Additionally, Afonso II set up a royal commission to investigate and recover properties that the church had acquired from the crown.

Sancho II ascended to the throne in 1223, completing the Reconquista in the Alentejo region. Contrary to what might be expected given his father, Afonso II's efforts to diminish the church's power, Sancho II found the church in a strong position. This could be due to various factors, such as the church's intervening events or political maneuvers, that negated or reversed Afonso II's efforts to curb its influence. His younger brother Afonso III became a count of Boulogne by marriage to the daughter of Raynald I of Dammartin-en-Goële. He was given the papal commission to take over after

Sancho. Pope Innocent IV deposed King Sancho in March 1245 due to his administrative negligence, conflicts with the clergy, and refusal to follow Roman Curia guidance, which led to his excommunication and the kingdom's instability. After a civil war that went on for two years, Sancho escaped to Toledo and passed on in 1248.

Afonso III, upon arrival, declared himself king. The death of Sancho II gave his usurpation legality. He united the divided kingdom and finished the reconquest of the Algarve. Afonso then relocated the capital from Coimbra to Lisbon. Bolstered by support from various towns, he convened a meeting of representatives from different municipalities to speak on behalf of the common people. His efforts to conquer the Algarve sparked jealousy in Castile, leading to military campaigns against him in 1250 and 1252. These conflicts were eventually settled through a marriage alliance. Despite already being married, he wed the daughter of Alfonso X of Castile. This marital union helped solidify his control over the Algarve, which ultimately became a permanent part of Portugal.

The marriage caused a dispute with the church, and Afonso III was put under interdict. Although he was subject to the Pope's authority, Afonso III chose not to comply with the Church's directives. In 1263, his marriage was eventually legalized, and his eldest son, Dinis, became legitimate. Although some high-ranking church officials attempted to object, the majority ended up leaving the country. Afonso III faced excommunication from the Catholic Church, a severe penalty that severed him from the sacraments and the religious community. This excommunication even put him at risk of losing his throne, as the Church threatened to depose him. Despite these severe sanctions and the immense influence of the Church, Afonso III remained defiant until his death in 1279, refusing to submit to the religious authority.

During the reign of King Dinis from 1279 to 1325, Portugal became increasingly integrated with Western Europe. The king promoted economic development by supporting market fairs and encouraging the use of minted currency, which in turn facilitated commercial growth. Additionally, Dinis took environmental measures, such as planting pine forests in Leiria to combat the encroachment of sand dunes. Dinis was interested in advancing agriculture and shipbuilding. In 1317, as one of his measures to stimulate foreign trade, he engaged an admiral, Emmanuele Pessagno, to build a naval force. King Dinis was instrumental in founding the University of Coimbra in 1290, and he was a patron of literature as well as a poet himself. However, King Dinis is also notably remembered for his innovative land management policies, such as planting the Leiria pine forest to combat soil erosion and provide timber resources, which have left a lasting impact on Portugal's environmental history.

Despite King Dinis's emphasis on internal development and peace, his reign was not without conflict; he faced border tensions with Castile, internal rebellions led by his brother Afonso, and disputes with the Catholic Church over jurisdictional and fiscal matters. In 1297, the Treaty of Alcañices confirmed that Portugal owned the Algarve and paved the way for the alliance between Castile and Portugal. Dinis and his wife Isabel, who was the daughter of Peter III of Aragon, had a son named Afonso IV. Isabel became known as St. Elizabeth of Portugal after being officially declared a saint. Often referred to as the "Holy Queen," she played a significant role in promoting peace during her husband Dinis's reign.

Afonso IV, who ruled from 1325 to 1357, was a courageous monarch frequently engaged in conflicts with Castile. His mother, Isabel, who had by that time retired to a convent in Coimbra, often stepped in to mediate and advocate for peace. However, after Isabel died in 1336, a war ensued that lasted for three years. The conflict concluded in 1340 when Afonso IV, leading his Portuguese army, joined forces with Alfonso

XI of Castile to defeat the Muslims in Andalusia. Peter I of Portugal, Afonso IV's son, initially married Constance of Castile, the daughter of Infante Juan Manuel. After her death, he began a romantic relationship with her cousin, Ines de Castro, with whom he had several children. Ines was controversially assassinated in 1355, a crime often attributed to orders from Peter's father, King Afonso IV. When Peter assumed the throne in 1357, one of his first acts was to seek vengeance for Ines' death. He ruled briefly from 1357 to 1367 and was noted for his stringent dispensation of justice. His harsh judgments were occasionally mitigated by his indulgence in revelry.

Ferdinand I, who ruled from 1367 to 1383, inherited a relatively stable and prosperous Portuguese throne. The primary external issue he faced was the ongoing conflict between the King of Castile and Henry II, both vying for control over the Castilian throne. Ferdinand I succeeded his father, Peter I, who died in 1367. Upon his ascension, several towns offered their allegiance to Ferdinand. While the historical details are not entirely clear, accepting these allegiances may have been considered unwise if Ferdinand was not prepared for the obligations or political complexities these allegiances might have entailed. In 1371, Ferdinand I chose to marry Leonor Teles, a Portuguese noblewoman, despite her already being married. Her previous marriage was annulled to allow the union, a decision fraught with political controversy. Sometime later, Ferdinand allied with John of Gaunt, the Duke of Lancaster, who claimed the throne of Castile through his marriage to Constance, the daughter of Peter of Castile. However, John of Gaunt never successfully ascended to the Castilian throne.

In 1372, facing hostilities with Henry II of Castile, Ferdinand I of Portugal found himself in a precarious position. Ultimately, he was compelled to abandon his alliance with John of Gaunt and sought terms with Castile, providing hostages as assurance. After the death of Henry II in 1379, Ferdinand once again explored alliances against Castile, this time with Edmund of Langley, the brother of John of Gaunt. Plans were made for a military campaign against Castile, and a marriage was arranged between Edmund's son and Ferdinand's only legitimate daughter, Beatriz. However, Ferdinand changed course amid these machinations and arranged for Beatriz to marry John I of Castile.

Ferdinand died in 1383, leaving his wife Leonor Teles as regent. His death ended the legitimate male line of the House of Burgundy in Portugal. This led to a succession crisis, with John I of Castile, now married to Beatriz, laying claim to the Portuguese throne. This would plunge Portugal into the 1383–1385 Crisis, eventually resolved in favor of a different Portuguese line, the House of Aviz.

Leonor Teles, the widow of Ferdinand I, was romantically involved with Juan Fernandes de Andeiro, a Galician nobleman who had political ties to both Castile and England. His influence was deeply unpopular among Portuguese patriots. As opposition against Castilian power grew, the patriots rallied around John, the master of Aviz, also a son of Peter I of Portugal. With solid backing from the citizens of Lisbon, John assumed the role of defender of Portugal.

Leonor Teles fled first to Alenquer and then to Santarem under the protection of the King of Castile. Eventually, she was placed in a Spanish convent. Lisbon came under Castilian siege in 1384, but the siege was lifted after five months due to an outbreak of plague among the Castilian forces. In April 1385, the Portuguese Cortes, a legislative assembly representing various estates of the realm, convened in Coimbra and formally recognized John of Aviz as king, establishing the House of Aviz as the new royal dynasty.

John of Aviz's appointment as king faced resistance from factions within the Portuguese clergy and nobility who viewed the Queen of Castile—Beatriz, the daughter of Ferdinand I of Portugal and wife to John I of Castile—as the legitimate heir to the throne. Despite this, popular sentiment largely favored John of Aviz. He also had key allies, including the Holy Constable and his military advisor, João das Regras. While some Portuguese castles and towns remained loyal to Castile, their resistance waned after the Portuguese army secured a decisive victory at the Battle of Aljubarrota in 1385. John of Aviz himself had a narrow escape during the battle.

The victory at the Battle of Aljubarrota solidified John I's hold on the Portuguese throne and strengthened his ties with England. A small contingent of English archers had participated in the battle on the Portuguese side. In recognition of this support, the Treaty of Windsor was signed in 1386, establishing a long-lasting alliance between England and Portugal. John of Gaunt, Duke of Lancaster, later visited the Iberian Peninsula but was unsuccessful in aiding John I in an invasion of Castile. Some historians argue that John I's ultimate success represented the triumph of national identity over feudal loyalties. Much of the old Portuguese nobility had sided with Castile, so John I rewarded his loyal supporters at the expense of the traditional aristocracy and the crown's resources.

The marriage of John I to Isabel of Portugal signifi-cantly impacted trade relations between Portugal and the County of Flanders, which Philip III ruled. This matrimonial alliance also set the stage for John to channel the ambitions of his sons and frontiersmen into overseas conquests, such as the capture of Ceuta in 1415. By 1437, John's eldest son, Edward, had succeeded him as king. During Edward's reign, Portugal unsuccessfully attempted to conquer Tangier, an endeavor later undertaken by Prince Henry the Navigator. When Edward died, his son Afonso V was still a child, leading to a regency headed by the Duke of Coimbra. However, the Duke's governance faced opposition, notably from the illegitimate descendants of John of Aviz and the influential Bragança family.

The Bragança family, who had become one of the most affluent and influential families in Portugal, successfully maneuvered to pit young King Afonso V against his uncle and regent, the Duke of Coimbra. This internal struggle culminated in the Duke's forced resignation from the regency, and he eventually died in the Battle of Alfarrobeira in 1449.

Afonso V, seemingly unable to resist the influence of the Bragança family, later married Joan, the daughter of Henry IV of Castile. This marital alliance led him into a prolonged conflict with Ferdinand and Isabella, the Catholic Monarchs of Spain, culminating in his defeat at the battles of Toro and Zamora in 1476. In a failed attempt to garner support, Afonso V traveled to France to seek the backing of Louis XI but returned unsuccessful. Subsequently, he agreed to the Treaty of Alcacovas, a move from which his reign never fully recovered.

These were the travails of Portugal's emergence as an independent kingdom. The attainment of its present borders did not happen before the mid-13th century. It may initially seem surprising that it took so long, but in terms of geography, Portugal is not exactly coherent. It consists of markedly different southern and northern regions that share more with Spain than with each other, and one can see why. Up until then, Portugal had never been recognized as a political entity. There was no unified language exclusive to the people and no awareness of a shared and distinct tradition.

In the broader context of the Reconquista, the formation of Portugal as an independent kingdom is more easily understood. As the Christian territories expanded, the challenges facing the Kings of Castile grew proportionally, leading them to exert control over peripheral areas like Coimbra and Portucale. These areas remained vulnerable to Muslim invasions but had developed critical military roles, enabling them to solidify their political power. Additionally, the leaders of these regions had accumulated significant economic and political advantages, and they hardened their family legacies through strategic intermarriages and prioritizing succession through adult male relatives over women or minors.

Undoubtedly, by the late medieval times, Portugal was an autonomous kingdom, but to what extent and how its people were born is subject to conjecture. One wonders how people born of feudal politics and the Reconquista developed an awareness of collective identity and a sense of nationhood. Portuguese historians have indeed grappled with this question. One fact remains, though—it seems undeniable that a Portuguese kingdom was essential as a prerequisite for the nation. The latter may never have developed without ever having been the former.

By the early 14th century, one key element of national identity was already in place: a national language. This language was a blend of various influences, including the Galician-Portuguese spoken during the reign of Afonso Henriques, Mozarab dialects, and Lusitano, along with the incorporation of numerous Arabic words. By the 13th century, during the rule of King Dinis, Portuguese had become increasingly prominent in official documents, effectively replacing Latin as the language of governance, while Latin remained the language of the church. Portugal was one of the first European states to make this linguistic transition.

The years between 1490 and 1540 stand out as a pivotal era in Portuguese history, often referred to by later generations as the 'golden age.' During these years, Portugal achieved unprecedented global influence. Portuguese explorers navigated around the Cape of Good Hope, established trading outposts from Brazil to Southeast Asia, and made significant contributions to the Age of Discovery. Domestically, the country managed to resolve long-standing political tensions and experienced economic growth, although there was some decline towards the end of this period. Notably, this era was also marked by significant contributions to art and literature, reflecting an overall sense of national optimism.

The early stages of Portugal's 'golden age' are closely tied to the Order of Aviz, a military order that played a significant role in Portuguese history. Portuguese independence was assured in 1385 when Portuguese forces defeated Castilian invaders at the Battle of Aljubarrota. This victory solidified Portugal's sovereignty and set the stage for the country's rise to prominence in the subsequent years. The Aviz dynasty governed Portugal for approximately two centuries, overseeing the nation's most illustrious era. The long-standing alliance with England, formalized through the Treaty of Windsor, was further strengthened when John I of Portugal married Philippa of Lancaster, an English noblewoman. Philippa played a significant role in enriching the cultural life of the Portuguese royal court.

John I had five sons, including Prince Henry, commonly known as Henry the Navigator (1394–1460). Prince Henry devoted his life to planning and sponsoring voyages of exploration. These expeditions altered the course of history and positioned Portugal as a leading nation in the age of global exploration and colonization. John II took power in 1481. His rule was firm and cautious, fueled by jealousy of the influence his father had neglected. In his inaugural meeting with the Cortes, the legislative assembly of Portugal, King John of Aviz presented an oath of homage that was poorly received by some of his most powerful vassals. Sensing their discontent could lead to a potential conspiracy against him, he took decisive action. He arrested Fernando II, the Duke of Bragança, and several of his supporters. This move sent a strong message about the king's determination to consolidate his power and authority, even if it meant creating tension among the nobility. He was sentenced to death, which was carried out in 1484 at Evora. In addition to attacking the nobility, John reduced the effects of the treaty with Castile, eventually earning him the name "the Perfect Prince."

Since John's son died before his father, John II was succeeded by his cousin, Manuel I, the Duke of Beja, who was called "the Fortunate." Manuel inherited the title "Lord of the Conquest, Commerce, and Navigation of Persia, Arabia, India and Ethiopia" from John II, as well as a firmly established monarchy, autocratic in nature, and rapidly growing overseas. Drawn toward Spain by the need to defend their interests overseas according to the Treaty of Tordesillas (1494), Manuel kept hope that the whole Peninsula could, at last, unite under the House of Aviz—hope which led him to marry Isabelle, Ferdinand's daughter. She, however, died in 1498 during childbirth and was survived by Miguel da Paz. Miguel was recognized as the heir to Castile, Aragon, and Portugal but died shortly after his mother. Manuel married Isabelle's sister, who died in 1517, and eventually Eleanor, Charles V's sister.

As part of the terms of his marriage to Isabelle, King Manuel I was obligated to remove Jews from Portugal. Previously, these Jews had been expelled from Spain in 1492 and were welcomed into Portugal by King John II, who taxed them heavily. Manuel gave the Jewish population until October 1497 to exit the country. During this waiting period, substantial efforts were made to convert them to Christianity through force or incentives. Those who refused to convert were permitted to leave the country. However, the Jews who converted were guaranteed that their new Christian faith would not be questioned for 20 years. As "new Christians," they couldn't be forced to move, and indeed, they evaded exodus from Portugal. In 1506, a devastating event occurred in Lisbon, Portugal, where many "new Christians" were brutally killed during a riot. Recognizing both the injustice done to them and possibly their economic value, he allowed them safe passage to Holland, where their trade experience benefited the Dutch.

King Manuel was unable to achieve his ambition of ruling Spain, and his son John III (who reigned from 1521 to 1557) similarly struggled to resist influence from Castile. John III was a devout and reserved man who allowed his wife, Catherine, to make important decisions. Catherine, the sister of Charles V, played a crucial role in establishing the Inquisition in Portugal. This religious body made its first public condemnation of heretics in an "act of faith" in 1536. Four years later, in 1540, the Society of Jesus, commonly known as the Jesuits, was founded. This religious order quickly gained control over education in Portugal.

During this period, geopolitical tensions extended beyond Europe as Portugal and Spain vied to control the Moluccas in present-day Indonesia. The territorial dispute was eventually resolved in 1529 through the

Treaty of Saragossa. This agreement clarified the spheres of influence for both empires, removing ambiguities that had hindered diplomatic relations between Spain and Portugal. It established boundaries in the Moluccas and extended a similar demarcation line across the Pacific, marking their respective colonial domains.

The geopolitical landscape was undergoing shifts within Europe during this time. While the Reformation altered religious and political dynamics across the continent, Portugal remained predominantly Catholic and was somewhat insulated from these religious upheavals. Nonetheless, alliances and relationships did evolve due to various factors, not just religious conflict.

4

THE AGE OF EASTERN AND WESTERN EXPLORATION VOYAGES AND THE DECLINE OF THE EMPIRE (1418–1520 AD)

While separated into two chapters in this book, Portugal under the Aviz dynasty coincided with the Western exploration voyages and the golden age. In 1418, Henry the Navigator established a center for maritime research in Sagres, located in the southwest of Portugal. He assembled a team of astronomers, sea captains, and cartographers to develop the fundamentals of open-sea navigation. Following this, he organized meticulously planned expeditions almost annually to gain geographical knowledge and establish trade routes with West Africa. For a long time, trade with the East was primarily controlled by Middle Eastern Arabs and was frequently disrupted by Moorish pirate attacks in the Mediterranean. Starting in the mid-15th century, the Turks began interfering with this trade. Their influence increased significantly after they conquered Constantinople in 1453.

Voyage groups discovered Madeira in 1419, the Azores in 1431, and Senegal in 1446. The Islands of Cape Verde were found in 1455. They brought gold back from West Africa and enslaved Africans to dig up Portugal's natural resources. Henry the Navigator passed in 1460, and his death produced a slackening of explorative activity. It was resumed in 1481 by King John II. In 1488, Bartholomew Diaz, a notable Portuguese explorer, became the first European to navigate around the southern tip of Africa. His achievement was a precursor to an even more monumental voyage by Vasco da Gama. Vasco da Gama, another prominent Portuguese explorer, set a new milestone between 1497 and 1498 by sailing around the southern tip of Africa to reach Calicut in India, taking a journey that lasted ten months. This expedition marked the pinnacle of Portugal's era of maritime exploration.

In 1500, Pedro Cabral, another Portuguese explorer, set out to establish trade relations with the East. During his journey, he landed in Brazil and then proceeded to the Indies. He transported a large shipment of spices back to Europe using Portuguese ships. Before this, spices were typically moved from the Spice Islands to Venice via Arab ships and overland routes. Cabral's voyages shifted the focus of the spice trade from Venice to Lisbon, making the Portuguese city the primary European hub for goods from the East. To safeguard and expand these lucrative trade routes, Portugal built an overseas empire in the eastern part of the world, led by figures such as Francisco de Almeida and Afonso de Albuquerque.

Almeida was born in 1450 in Lisbon and became a soldier, explorer, and then the first Viceroy of Portuguese India. After gaining some fame in the wars against the Moors, Manuel I appointed him as Viceroy of the newly conquered Indian territories. Leaving with a powerful fleet of twenty-one ships, he rounded the Cape of Good Hope, sailed up the east coast, took present-day Tanzania, constructed a port, and destroyed Mombasa (Kenya) before proceeding to India to live in Cochin. Determined to see Portugal become the paramount eastern power with a monopoly on the spice trade, he created a series of outposts. Under his administration, a treaty for commerce was concluded in Malacca (present-day Malaysia) to govern trade. His son Lourenco would later continue his explorations.

When Arabs and their Egyptian allies later challenged Portuguese dominance, Almeida burned and pillaged their ports, defeating their fleet off Diu, India, in 1509. Almeida had had his fair share of exploits when Afonso de Albuquerque arrived in Cochin to supersede him. Still, he doubted Afonso's commission and imprisoned him. In 1509, he was forced to recognize Afonso's authority and the legality of his claim. He set sail for Portugal and was killed in a skirmish with Khoekhoe. After taking over as Viceroy, Albuquerque took Goa on the Indian west coast in 1510. Goa went on to become the capital of Portuguese India. He began attempts to conquer Ceylon, now known as Sri Lanka, a region that Almeida had previously explored.

Gradually, the Portuguese took over Ceylon from the natives. Portugal was now the master of the Indian Ocean. In 1511, Albuquerque captured Malacca from its Muslim rulers, obtaining another strategic trading center and setting Portugal up to dominate the trade route to the Far East. The Portuguese aimed to gain control over the Spice Islands but faced opposition from Spain. Afonso de Albuquerque, whose paternal grandfather and great-grandfather had served as secretaries to King John I, had a specific strategy. He planned to construct permanent fortifications to establish a robust Portuguese presence in the Orient, drawing on the administrative skills he had learned from a young age.

Afonso de Albuquerque had an extensive military background before making his mark in Asia. He had spent a decade serving in North Africa, where he gained experience fighting against Muslim forces. He was part of the Portuguese army that helped King Afonso V capture Tangier in 1471. Later, he served under King John II, who appointed him Master of the Horse, a title he continued to hold when he was in India.

In 1489, Albuquerque was involved in defending Graciosa in North Africa under the reign of King Manuel I. Although his influence may have waned by this point, it was in the East where he truly established his reputation. After Vasco da Gama's successful voyage around the Cape of Good Hope to India, King Manuel sent additional fleets to establish relations with Indian rulers. Before the Portuguese arrived, Muslim traders dominated the spice trade and resisted Portuguese attempts to break their monopoly.

In 1503, Afonso de Albuquerque established the first Portuguese fortress in Asia and staffed it with a garrison. He then set up a trading post in Quilon, present-day Kerala, India. After these accomplishments, he returned to Lisbon in 1504 to assist in shaping official policy. Later, Albuquerque constructed fortresses on the island of Socotra, located near the Horn of Africa, to disrupt Arab trade routes. In 1507, he opened Persian trade with Europe after capturing the Persian Gulf and the Gulf of Oman. While Afonso de

Albuquerque was in the process of succeeding Francisco de Almeida in command, his son was killed by an Egyptian navy. In response, Albuquerque took on the leadership role and vowed to maintain it until he had avenged his son's death. Although he had already been slated to assume a significant position, this personal tragedy intensified his resolve. His initial attempt to capture Cochin was unsuccessful. Reevaluating his strategy, he led a fleet of twenty-three ships to attack Goa, where he successfully defeated the Muslim defenders, leaving no survivors.

After defeating the Muslims, the Hindu rulers acknowledged the permanent presence of the Portuguese in India. Albuquerque then utilized Goa as a military base against Muslim forces and as a supply route to Hindu provinces. He married his men to the local women so that Goa would get a new population with an assured supply of goods. It was after winning Goa that he set forth to conquer Malacca. While he sent ships there, Goa came under heavy attack, and in 1512, Albuquerque was forced to retreat. Finding Socotra to be an inadequate base, Albuquerque attempted to capture Aden, a strategic port city in present-day Yemen, but was unsuccessful. He explored Abyssinian and Arabian coasts as a final resort until he eventually subdued Calicut.

In 1515, Albuquerque departed from Goa, intending to seize control of Hormuz, an island strategically located at the entrance of the Persian Gulf. However, he fell ill and was forced to return to Goa, where he discovered that Lope Soares, a personal adversary, had taken over his position. He died a bitter man on the ship before reaching Goa, but his plans, derived from John II's crusading spirit, were kept alive by other leaders who followed him. Worthy mentioning is Ferdinand Magellan, a man who served under Albuquerque but later fell out with the authorities in Portugal. Magellan transferred his allegiance to Spain and, in 1519, sent by his new masters, went to the East Indies through South America. He died in the Philippines during a conflict with local inhabitants. Still, some members of his fleet, led by Sebastian del Cano—who would later become famous for completing the first circumnavigation of the globe—managed to reach the Molucca Islands.

The rivalry between Portugal and Spain in the Moluccas ended in favor of Portugal, and Spain turned its efforts to the Philippines. Within twenty years, between 1564 and 1584, Spain conquered most of the Philippine islands from their Muslim rulers during ongoing eastern colonization. Meanwhile, Portugal obtained Macao from China in 1557. Britain would later take control of Macao approximately 300 years after Portugal first acquired it. Portugal had initially obtained Macao as a reward for combating piracy in Chinese waters. However, it's worth noting that Macao is no longer a Portuguese possession; it was returned to China in 1999. Nevertheless, Portugal was the first European country to establish an empire in the East.

In the vicinity of the European mainland, Portugal had acquired the Cape Verde Islands, Azores, and Madeira. During the 16th century, Portugal expanded its colonial reach into Africa, initially focusing on Mozambique and later Angola. The primary aim of these African colonies was originally trade. Over time, Portugal established settlements and forts, extending its influence further into the African interior. This often led to conflicts with native communities as Portugal sought to annex strategic locations. Concurrently, both Portugal and Spain continued expanding their influence in the Western Hemisphere.

A sailor who settled in Portugal in 1478, Christopher Columbus participated in many Portuguese exploration voyages. He was convinced that you could reach Asia if you sailed westwards, so in the 1480s, he called upon King John of Portugal to allow him the resources to go on such a voyage. Portugal was already very committed to West Africa and was looking for an African route to take them east, so King John declined the proposal. After approaching England unsuccessfully in 1492,

Columbus secured the backing of Isabella and Ferdinand of Spain.

He had a fleet of three tiny ships. Ten weeks into the voyage, after prevailing over some misgivings from his crew, he struck land in the West Indies. Columbus named the land San Salvador, believing until the end of his voyages that he had discovered India. Fearing Portugal would launch a counterclaim, Isabella and Ferdinand quickly claimed rights to the new land. The pope, then a Spaniard, was given possession of all territories beyond the line drawn west of the Cape Verde Islands and the Azores. This decision was not well-received by other European nations, and it had no bearing on the colonization of North America. However, it prevented a dispute between Portugal and Spain. The Treaty of Tordesillas later amended this arrangement by moving the dividing line 270 leagues west, granting Portugal possession of its coastal regions.

Thus, Portugal was in possession of Brazil. It officially took control in 1500 after the explorer Cabral landed there. Columbus made a few more western voyages, each making him hungrier for the next. He inspired others after him to go on expeditions, the most famous being Ferdinand Magellan's and those of Amerigo Vespucci. Vespucci was a Florentine who first served

Spain before voyaging in service of Portugal between 1499 and 1502. Two significant documents describe his voyages in detail. The first one is a letter named Vespucci of Lisbon, Portugal, dated as far back as the 4th of September, 1504. Written in Italian, expectedly to the magistrate of medieval Italy, Piero Soderini, the letter was first printed in Florence a year later. There are two Latin versions of the same letter.

The second series has three private letters, all written to the Medici. The first one mentions four Vespucci voyages, the second one only two. For the longest time, the first letter was considered to be from the perspective of the order to undertake the voyages. Alberto Magnaghi theorized the contrary, saying that the documents resulted from skillful manipulations. To him, the only authentic papers were the private letters. If that is the case, Vespucci went on two voyages instead of four. Answering that question matters to how you talk about the man's work and his contribution to historical Portugal. Attempts to reconcile the two sets of letters have not been universally accepted.

In 1500, Vespucci completed a voyage as the navigator of a fleet of four ships sent from Spain and led by Alonso de Ojeda. Since he acted as a navigator, we can conclude that it does seem possible that he went on other voyages before this one. On the journey, Vespucci left Ojeda after arriving at the coast of modern-day Guyana. Turning south, he is suspected of having found the mouth of the Amazon River and gone as far as Cape St. Augustine. While coming back, he reached Trinidad, saw the mouth of River Orinoco, and then set sail for Haiti. Historically, it's believed that he thought he was navigating along the coast of the Asian Peninsula, where the ancient geographer Ptolemy had placed a location called Cattigara. He assumed that once his ships passed this point, they would emerge in southern Asia.

When Vespucci returned to Spain, he requested to be equipped and sent on another expedition to reach the Gulf of the Ganges (present-day Bay of Bengal) and present-day Sri Lanka. The Spanish government was not thrilled about his proposal, so it declined. By the end of the year 1500, Vespucci began working in the service of Portugal. For Portugal, he completed another expedition that stopped at the Cape Verde Islands and traveled southwest to Brazil. The rest of this voyage is disputed, but he claimed to have traveled south to Rio de Janeiro Bay and then to the Rio de la Plata, making him the first European to discover the estuary. His ships may have continued south along the coasts of present-day Argentina. There is no record of his return route, but his ships anchored at Lisbon in 1502.

On the other hand, Magellan first sailed to Brazil before exploring the Rio de la Plata estuary while looking for a western passage. Failing at his mission, he continued south and passed the Strait of Magellan (his namesake) through the Pacific into the East Indies. In 1504, when Queen Isabella of Castile died, it destabilized Spain's throne. A couple of years later, after the death of King Ferdinand of Aragon, the throne passed to Charles I, their grandson. Charles inherited Spain together with her colonies in America and southern Italy. His paternal grandfather was Emperor Maximilian I of Hapsburg, and he inherited the Netherlands and Austria from him. In 1519, he was elected as the Holy Roman Emperor, which made him Emperor Charles V and added Germany to his empire.

By birth, Charles was a Fleming. He was only nineteen when he took over a diverse and vast empire. Having little imagination or charm, Charles' saving grace was his perseverance, quickness in understanding, and good intentions. Still, the problems that came his way, including the German Reformation and France's hostility, were tremendous. During his reign, the empire experienced periodic wars, first against France and then against the protestants in Germany. Though he would have preferred compromise and conciliation with the protestants, he was inevitable, because of his Spanish and Habsburg background, the papal champion. Spain became the crux of his power, though his Spanish subjects were unhappy that he used their wealth for imperial campaigns. His regular absences also became a problem.

In 1555, worn out from his responsibilities as emperor, Charles V abdicated the throne and retired to a monastery in Spain. He was succeeded as Holy Roman Emperor by his brother, Ferdinand. Meanwhile, his son Philip ascended to the throne as Philip II of Spain, taking control of Spain's colonial empire, southern Italy, and the Netherlands. He was serious and hard-working but incredibly narrow-minded, keeping him in bureaucratic details. He thought of himself as a defender of Catholicism. Spain enjoyed most of its golden age while Philip II was king, becoming the strongest European power. Its main strength was its infantry, primarily volunteers from noble families.

However, there was a weak link in its armor. Spain divided its naval resources between the Mediterranean to combat the Ottoman Empire, and the Atlantic. Allied with the Papal and Venetian fleets, it managed a decisive victory over the Turks in 1571, confirming it as the champion of Christendom. However, despite its vast stake in America, it had no sustained domination effort in the Atlantic. By discouraging its colonies from foreign trade, Spain failed to realize its potential for wealth. This, coupled with an ineffective taxation system at home, which left the wealthy clergy immune and created a lot of speculation, left it perpetually broke.

Because of these financial difficulties, Spain increasingly relied on the Netherlands as its primary source of income. Complicating matters further was the heavy-handed presence of the Spanish Inquisition, which led to a Dutch revolt. In 1567, Philip II sent the Duke of Alva to the Netherlands with a Spanish army to quash the rebellion. However, by that time, many in the Netherlands had adopted Calvinism, a branch of Protestant Christianity that emphasized the sovereignty of God and predestination, and the Duke's severe methods only served to heighten existing tensions. After failing to subdue the Dutch rebellion, Spain sent the Duke of Parma, a skilled diplomat and military leader, to handle the situation. He managed to win support in the southern parts of the Netherlands and achieved a significant victory near Brussels in 1578. As a result, the southern provinces remained under Spanish rule, becoming known as the Spanish Netherlands.

In the north, though, the Dutch would not relent. They were kept alive by their mastery of the seas. Meanwhile, relations with the protestants in England had worsened. In 1553, Philip married Queen Mary of England. After her death, Queen Elizabeth ascended to the throne, effectively thwarting Philip's aspirations for a Catholic Europe. A constant war threat between England and Spain was made worse by England's support of the Dutch. Five years later, Philip took action to challenge England by initiating an invasion using Spain's naval fleet, known as the Spanish Armada. However, the fleet was utterly defeated by the English. In the years that followed, the Dutch showed that Spanish fleets and armies were not invincible, and after a couple of severe defeats, Spain gave up the struggle, agreeing to a truce with the Dutch, who had claimed their independence earlier on.

Meanwhile, Portugal, declining from the height of its glory, looked less formidable. Manuel I repeated the mistake already made by Spain of expelling the Jews without realizing that Portugal's prosperity relied on them. When John III, his son, took over, militant Catholicism greatly influenced the country. In 1536, the Inquisition was established to root out heresy. Earlier, Ignatius of Loyola, a Basque, had founded the Jesuit order, which received official approval from the Pope in 1540. The Jesuits became key players in the Catholic Counter-Reformation. Their primary roles included combating heresy, conducting global missionary work, and addressing ignorance and corruption within the clergy. They established schools emphasizing education and rigorous discipline to achieve the latter goal.

In particular, the Jesuits strategically aimed their efforts at individuals who wielded significant influence, thereby acquiring some degree of political power themselves. Having been educated by Jesuits, King Sebastian represented a high point for the order's influence within the Portuguese government. Despite this promising start, Sebastian's ill-fated crusade against the Moors led to a devastating loss at Alcácer Quibir in 1578, which shattered the Portuguese army and claimed Sebastian's life, along with much of the Portuguese nobility.

Sebastian's great-uncle Henry, a cardinal, succeeded him, but his death eventually ended the Aviz dynasty. Multiple claimants, including Philip II of Spain, eyed the Portuguese throne at this juncture. With the support of the Jesuits, Philip's armies, commanded by the Duke of Alba, invaded Portugal. After securing a pivotal victory at Alcantara in 1580, Philip was crowned king of Portugal. For the subsequent six decades, Portugal existed under Spanish dominion, with its interests often taking a back seat to those of Spain.

5

THE SHORT-LIVED IBERIAN UNION AND PORTUGAL'S INDEPENDENCE (1580–1640 AD)

After Philip became Portugal's king, by his decree, Portugal would be governed through a council with six members. The Portuguese Cortes would now only meet in Portugal, and all ecclesiastical, military, and civil appointments would remain Portuguese, with an autonomous military, coinage, language, and judicial system. He supported two Portuguese institutions which he thought would unite Spain and Portugal—the Inquisition and the Jesuits. As a result, new Christians were persecuted even more. Understanding Philip's decisions and mindset becomes significantly clearer when considering his early life and experiences before ascending to the Portuguese throne.

In 1522, before the era of Philip II, Emperor Charles V returned to Spain after extensive travels through his

European territories, including the Holy Roman Empire. During his time in Germany, he had to contend with the rise of Martin Luther and the Protestant Reformation. Despite his far-reaching responsibilities, Charles V remained actively involved in Spanish affairs. Upon returning to Spain, he learned of the Comuneros Rebellion, a popular uprising against his rule. Initially, he considered making a harsh example out of the rebels through executions but ultimately chose a path of reconciliation. He offered pardons and took steps to address the grievances that had led to the uprising. These actions marked a shift in his approach to governance, as he had previously been criticized for being insensitive to the needs and concerns of his Spanish subjects. Over the following months, he worked to rectify his earlier mistakes, making concessions that responded to the demands that had sparked the revolt.

High on the list of demands was that he marry within the realm. The deputies to the Cortes hoped that he'd marry Isabel, sister to Portugal's king, and he eventually obliged. It was a political union, but he fell in love with his wife, and in 1527, a son was born to them. Isabel was in labor for thirteen hours, and Charles remained by her side the whole time. The infant, Philip, was born into a politically turbulent environment and welcomed with grand celebrations. Just a year earlier, his father

Charles had released Francis I of France, whom he had previously captured. Additionally, Pope Clement was challenging Charles' authority in Milan. Due to these pressing state affairs, Charles was not heavily involved in raising his son, who was acknowledged as the heir to the throne of Castile.

Every facet of Philip's upbringing was meticulously managed. His mother, Isabel, had a Portuguese circle of influence, instilling a lifelong affinity for Portuguese culture in Philip. While his father, Charles, was often preoccupied with state matters, he remained concerned about Philip's well-being, inquiring regularly about his health. As a child, Philip was mischievous, occasionally exasperating his mother, but their relationship was generally positive. Although she passed away when he was young, he looked up to her as a role model for behavior and character.

In 1534, after Charles returned to Spain, Philip received a comprehensive education. He was assigned a Parisian priest as a tutor, appointed a new governor, and given a separate household. Educational materials, including books on grammar and reading, were explicitly prepared for him. Despite periodic interruptions due to illness, by 1540, Philip had achieved a level of proficiency in his studies that surpassed many children of his age.

Philip's nonacademic interests included things like hunting and jousting. In 1541, Philip received another tutor who focused on mathematics and architecture, trying to get the prince to his father's desired level of academic excellence. Even though his tutors often addressed him in Latin, he would respond in Spanish. He refused to become a scholar even though he grew up grounded in literature, reading Petrarch, Sophocles, Vitruvio, and Copernicus, among others. His major problem growing up was his father's absence, but he soon started participating in Cortes meetings briefly before his father dismissed them. Considering his circumstances, it isn't easy to believe Philip received affection at home. His father was an object of reverence rather than love, and his mother died when he was only twelve.

Lacking a loving childhood was not uncommon for princes—they were often raised as men instead of children. Emotional attachments, such as love, were considered inappropriate for politicians. Even so, Philip did not become overly serious. He enjoyed the distractions and pleasures of young men. In 1542, Philip became betrothed to his cousin, Maria Manuela, Princess of Portugal, and the two were married in 1543. Philip was assigned a separate household staffed by 110 people, primarily the sons of bureaucrats and aristocrats. While he became familiar with Castile's staff and key towns, his knowledge of other parts of Spain remained limited until he accompanied his father on a royal tour through Aragon, Valencia, and Catalonia.

Little by little, Philip became the effective ruler of Spain. His early years of regency were the only apprenticeship he got, but they shaped him for his reign. In 1543, Philip took up his new role as governor of Aragon. He was still studying but was more involved in the councils' business, which he proved good at. In those days, the government was a bit simpler than today. The state's reach was limited, and there was no proper bureaucracy. The king's primary duties involved raising taxes, maintaining peace, or waging war. Philip increasingly turned to advisors to help him make decisions as his responsibilities grew. By the end of the year, Philip became interested in affairs concerning the Americas and was able to implement some policies that he favored.

At only sixteen years old, Philip began holding formal audiences, with one of his earliest guests being the Marquis of Mondejar. Now the undisputed ruler of Spain, he implemented a new procedure allowing individual opinions to be formally presented, aiding his decision-making process. Throughout his reign, he remained committed to considering a range of perspectives before making decisions.

Perhaps because of Philip's history and competence, or perhaps because of the Papal backing, Portuguese nobility did not dispute the incorporation of Portugal into a union with Spain. The royal court had been using the customs and language of Castile for many years now. Much work had already been done in Castile by writers from Portugal, who were aware that they belonged to a unified Iberian culture. However, in the countryside, things were different. There was a current of resistance driven by a messianic cult of Sebastian, the "hidden prince."

Sebastian, believed to be the heir to the Portuguese throne, took power in 1568 and was educated by Jesuits. Ignoring advice from family, he pursued a costly crusade against Morocco in 1578, where he and his army were defeated, and he died. The myth sprang up that he never died in the battle. There are records of up to four impostors who claimed to be him.

Either way, members of the cult believed that Sebastian did not die at Alcacer Quibir. They expected he would return and deliver Portugal from Spain's domination. The cult grew and became deeply rooted in time, and some impostors between 1584 and 1598 were responsible for sparking rebellions against Philip. The uprisings were quickly put down, but to date, Sebastianism, or the undying nostalgic longing for what is unattainable, is part of Portuguese culture.

During Philip II's reign, the terms of the union proclamation between the two crowns were upheld. In 1598, Philip II died, and his son, Philip III, ascended to the Spanish throne. Philip III did not have as much respect for Portugal's autonomy as his father did. He did not even visit Portugal until 1619, toward the end of his reign. When he took over, he started appointing Spaniards to the Cortes and the six-member council set up by his father and other lesser Portuguese posts. Philip III's reign was between 1598 and 1621. It was characterized mainly by foreign policy for peace in Spain's western European territories, the expulsion of the Moriscos (Muslims who had converted to Christianity but were suspected of practicing Islam in secret) internally, and a government filled with the king's trusted advisors, who focused on consolidating power and managing domestic and international challenges.

Before becoming king, Philip III was known for his kindness, strong moral character, and devoutness. However, once he took the throne, he lacked interest in his duties and became notably inactive. Before his death, his father had hinted at his disappointment with his son, describing him as unfit to govern God's kingdoms. As his father predicted, Philip III would be governed by his kingdoms. In 1599, he married Archduchess Margaret of Austria. Initially, he gave only his favorite people responsibility over state affairs. Thanks to him, the Duke of Lerma, Marques de Denia, and Gomez de Sandoval became the first people in a line of royal favorites to govern Spain and Portugal in the 17th century.

During his reign, Philip III maintained a policy of hostility towards the Turks. He also faced a rivalry between the Duke of Savoy and the Republic of Venice. Nonetheless, he successfully upheld a conciliatory Spanish policy towards the rest of Western Europe. That Western peace enabled his government to deal with the internal issues with the Moriscos and, eventually, strengthened the decision to expel them, which still caused a major demographic and economic problem. Peace was achieved with the conclusion of the Thirty Years' War, during which he had offered unwavering support to Ferdinand II and the Catholic German princes.

For the entirety of his reign, Philip III was largely detached from his subjects and the pressing issues facing Spain, such as the deteriorating economy. In 1619, he visited Madrid and Portugal before passing away in 1621. His son, Philip IV, succeeded him with similarly little enthusiasm for governance. This lack of attention had negative consequences for Portugal. Philip IV handed over the kingdom's administration to his advisor, Gaspar de Guzmán, known as the Duke of Olivares. Olivares implemented policies that eroded Portuguese autonomy and angered people across all social classes in Portugal. To bolster Spain's waning power, Olivares levied heavy taxes and conscripted troops from Portugal to support Spanish military campaigns, particularly against France. Interestingly, while his policies sowed division, Olivares harbored ambitions of administratively uniting Spain and Portugal. This goal seemed at odds with his actions, as they only fueled resentment and ultimately contributed to Portugal's quest for independence.

In 1637, a rebellion broke out in Evora when Spanish officials tried to collect levied taxes by force. Portuguese nobles had been called to Madrid and instructed to recruit soldiers to join the war against France. Expectedly, they were not pleased. Encouraged by Cardinal Richelieu of France, who promised to support them with ships and soldiers, they started to conspire against the Spanish. During that rebellion, the populace chose João, the Duke of Bragança, to be king. The duke was the closest noble to the House of Aviz and was Portugal's largest landowner and leading aristocrat. The nobility backed the populace's choice and conspired to have João become king.

In 1640, inspired by a Catalan revolt against Philip IV, supporters of João, the Duke of Bragança, took decisive action. They stormed the royal palace in Lisbon and arrested the Spanish governor, the Duchess of Mantua, who was also a relative of Philip IV. Within just five days, the Duke of Bragança arrived in Lisbon and was crowned King João IV of Portugal. This marked the restoration of the Portuguese monarchy and the establishment of a new ruling dynasty: the House of Bragança. These events were a culmination of years of discontent with Spanish rule, fueled in part by heavy taxation and military conscription imposed by the Duke of Olivares, Philip IV's chief advisor. The restoration of the Portuguese monarchy provides essential context for understanding the period from 1580 to 1640 from Spain's perspective.

Spain gained some additional strength when it united with Portugal in 1580. Nevertheless, the nation's waning influence in Europe, a decline that started with the unsuccessful attempt to conquer the Dutch using its naval fleet, the Armada, in 1588, persisted. With its finances in disarray, agriculture failing, and Portugal growing discontent by the day, Spain needed a time of retrenchment and peace. Spain needed time to eliminate corruption and address internal political scheming. However, the country sought to maintain a significant role in European politics instead of focusing on these internal issues. So, between 1589 and 1598, it intervened on the Catholic side of the religious civil war in France. When Philip II died in 1598, and his two successors appeared to have little interest in politics, Spain struggled.

The Duke of Olivares attempted to persuade Philip IV that achieving victory in a significant conflict could restore Spain's lost prestige. After a 12-year truce with the Dutch ended in 1621, Spain re-entered that conflict and became involved in another major European war, known as the Thirty Years' War, which lasted from 1618 to 1648. The war began as a struggle between Protestant and Catholic European nations. In its last phase, it turned purely political, mainly featuring Protestant Holland and Sweden and Catholic France on one side and Catholic Spain and Austria and Protestant Germany on the other. The war policy by Olivares didn't achieve anything more than disaster. In 1639, Portuguese and Spanish fleets were destroyed by the Dutch in a battle off the coast of Kent in the English Channel.

Soon after the conflict ended, the Treaty of Westphalia was established, granting the Dutch their own independent nation. This treaty effectively ended the Thirty Years' War and established the principles of state sovereignty in Europe. Still, Spain's war with France went on for another eleven years, and during that time, Cromwell's England took the side of France. Jamaica was captured from Spain during an English expedition, and English troops stepped in to help France beat Spain in the Spanish Netherlands (current-day Belgium) near Dunkirk in 1658. When the Treaty of the Pyrenees was signed a year later, it shifted the balance of power by firmly establishing France, not Spain, as the leading nation in Europe. The treaty settled territorial disputes in France's favor and marked a decline in Spanish influence, elevating France as the dominant European power.

Meanwhile, Olivares' policy of power centralization in Spain, coupled with high taxation, led to a revolt by the Catalans in the northeast in 1640. Before then, the Catalans had enjoyed a significant measure of autonomy. France supported the revolution, but it took twelve years before Barcelona finally submitted to Spanish authority.

Thanks to the Treaty of the Pyrenees, the Catalans kept most of the privileges they had enjoyed before. The Catalonian revolt strengthened the Portuguese, and they followed with their own uprising. The sixty years of union with Spain had not benefited Portugal in any way. Instead, Portugal had been dragged into Spain's wars in Europe, which it was not interested in. Cádiz had inherited some of the trading activity from Lisbon, and Portugal had even lost its position as the leading Eastern maritime power to the Dutch. Olivares' centralization of authority and heavy taxation rubbed salt into the wound. He was even planning to use Portuguese troops to quell the Catalan rebellion. All of these factors contributed to the success of the 1640 Portuguese revolt. With the overwhelming support of the people and the nobility, the Duke of Bragança became king.

Of course, the transition was not simple. The warfare resulted in embittered relations between Spain and Portugal and continued for twenty-eight years until, in 1668, Spain recognized Portugal as an independent nation. However, Portugal had lost Malacca, Ceylon, and the Moluccas to the Dutch, meaning it only had Goa, Macao, and part of the East Indies in its eastern possessions. In the Portuguese-controlled region of South America, the Dutch had captured Pernambuco, an important colonial territory in Brazil, and had expanded their influence further into the country. They defeated the Portuguese fleet sent to remedy the situation and take over Brazil. Additionally, the French and the English had already started colonizing the north coast, an area in Brazil where Portugal had shown interest.

During the 16th and 17th centuries, the political and military power of Spain and, by association, Portugal waned. However, this era also marked a golden age for both countries in the fields of literature and art. Today, we hear of renowned artists like Ribero, Murillo, and Velasquez. During Portugal's decline from its peak influence, poets like Camoens emerged. He wrote about Portugal's golden era of exploration, capturing the spirit of a time when the country was a dominant force. He died the same year Portugal achieved independence from Spain—his rumored last words were, "I am dying together with my country."

Portugal's seaborne empire may have declined before the Iberian Union, but the Spanish captivity sped up the process. The Portuguese were dragged into Spain's wars with Holland and England, a move that caused attacks on their Asian holdings and the eventual capture of Brazil from their possessions. Portugal lost its commercial monopoly in the East, specifically in regions like Southeast Asia, to the Dutch while losing its influence in India to the English. By the time they regained independence, the empire was significantly reduced.

6

THE HOUSE OF BRAGANÇA AND THE RESTORATION (1641–1730 AD)

The House of Bragança is a royal dynasty that originated in Portugal and produced kings, emperors, and other nobles who influenced Europe and the Americas. The dynasty was founded by Afonso I, the first Duke of Bragança, an illegitimate son of King John I of Portugal from the House of Aviz. The House of Bragança gained prominence and wealth in the Iberian Peninsula, particularly during the Renaissance. In 1640, during the Portuguese Restoration War, the Duke of Bragança was crowned King John IV of Portugal, ousting the Spanish Habsburg rule under Philip IV and restoring Portuguese independence. The reign of the House of Bragança extended to the Algarves (both in Europe and Africa), Brazil, and Portugal, unifying these territories under its rule.

In Portugal, the House provided fifteen monarchs and many consorts to different kingdoms in Europe, like Catherine of Bragança (married to England's Charles II and responsible for introducing tea to Britain) and Maria Isabel of Bragança (married to Ferdinand VII of Spain and said to have founded the El Prado Museum in Madrid). The House also supplied candidates for various royal thrones, such as those in Greece and Poland. It produced other significant individuals who played important roles in the Americas and Europe's history. The Braganças would eventually be deposed from their American and European thrones at the beginning of the 20th century when Emperor Pedro II was overthrown in Brazil and King Manuel II in Portugal.

After the reign of John VI, a Portuguese monarch and son of Queen Maria I (or Maria the Pious), the House of Bragança was divided into three major family branches. One branch was established in Brazil under Pedro I of Brazil. Another followed constitutional governance led by Portugal's Queen Maria II, and a third, known as the Miguelist branch, was under King Miguel I of Portugal. The branch of the family in Brazil evolved into the House of Orleans-Bragança. Much later, two factions within this Brazilian house would conflict over leadership. The constitutional branch was phased out with the death of King Manuel II in 1932, so the claim to the throne of Portugal was left to the Miguelist branch. The crown in Portugal passed to Duarte Pio, the most recognized pretender to the throne.

At the cradle of this influential house, in the mid-to-late 15th century, Afonso I could accomplish all he did because his father valued him beyond his illegitimacy. This is illustrated by his arrangement of Afonso's marriage to Beatriz, the daughter of Nuno Alvares Pereira, then the most important Portuguese general and the king's personal friend. The marriage augmented his social status and made him the head of a well-established house. He became eighth in line for the Count of Barcelo's title, an honor later ceded to him by his in-law, whom the king had made the seventh count. Thus, the roots of the House of Bragança were laid.

With his new place among the nobility in Portugal, Afonso started what would be a highly successful social and political career. In 1415, he participated in the Conquest of Ceuta with his brothers, father, and some members of the military and nobility. While the story of the Conquest of Ceuta chronologically fits in with Chapter 4 of this book, the details of the conquest feature here for the sake of context.

At the dawn of the Portuguese Empire, the House of Bragança played a crucial role in transforming Portugal from a struggling European nation into the creator of the world's first long-distance maritime empire. This empire came to dominate the Indian Ocean and almost monopolized global trade. This remarkable achievement can largely be attributed to exceptional individuals' audacity, vision, and unwavering determination, many of whom belonged to the Bragança family.

In 1415, 200 ships and 40,000 Portuguese men gathered in the Algarve port and crossed the Straits of Gibraltar to conquer the port of Ceuta in Morocco. Among these men was Afonso I of Bragança. Ceuta was the first acquisition and the inspiration behind the Portuguese empire, and its capture shook Europe. Ceuta was one of the Mediterranean's most fortified and strategically crucial ports. In contrast, Portugal was not a particularly affluent kingdom during this period, mainly focusing on agriculture and fishing. However, Portuguese leaders knew of Ceuta's significance as a trading hub for valuable goods like gold and spices from Africa and the Orient. The port served as a critical stopover point for caravans transporting these commodities.

Besides the economic incentives, there was a strategic objective for Portugal. It wanted control over the Straits of Gibraltar to have a base to fight Muslim pirates and battle Islamic power in the region, creating a way to unite Christendom. There was Christian tradition in the Peninsula and the goal of Reconquista, which was necessary for the Christians. Some parts of the Peninsula still embraced Islam, and Islamic invasions were constantly threatened, like the one in 1340, fought by Castilian and Portuguese forces. Back then, an agreement between the kings of Castile, Portugal, and Aragon had allowed them to conquer their neighboring Islamic kingdoms—and for Portugal, that was Morocco. After the battle, it became a Portuguese goal always to fight Islam.

The tradition of Reconquista was so deeply embedded in Portuguese culture that, between 1341 and 1377, Portuguese kings obtained five papal bulls that permitted them to conduct crusades against Muslims, either in North Africa or Granada. Because of the Black Death, which was rampant at the time, and the wars between Castile and Portugal, Portugal could not conduct those crusades. In 1411, Portugal established peace with Castile, and the impact of the Black Death subsided. This stability allowed Portugal to commit to its crusades against Islamic targets fully. Initially, Granada was the intended target for Portugal, but a subsequent agreement among the three ruling kings made it inaccessible. As a result, Portugal shifted its focus to capturing Ceuta instead.

The Portuguese army was commanded by King John I and his sons Henrique, Pedro, and Duarte, and they launched a surprise attack on Ceuta. King John I founded the House of Aviz that had previously ruled Portugal. During an era when the ideals of chivalry held significant importance, he took to the battlefield alongside his male relatives. In this period, honor was most highly esteemed when earned in combat, and there was no greater glory for a warrior than vanquishing Moorish forces. Some Crusaders were experienced soldiers, but others were too young to have ever gone to war. While some warriors were eager and relentless, driven by a desire to earn their spurs and attain honor, others may have been gripped by fear, trembling at the prospect of battle.

Whatever the case, wars were vicious, bloody, and brutal. Some men prayed for a fast and painless death instead of being mortally wounded and dying slowly. Others prayed that they did not become prisoners of war. Prisoners were shown no mercy. Most of them died by torture or were sold as enslaved people. These men knew they faced a considerable possibility of death by a merciless enemy. Before battle, the priest assigned to each ship would stand before the assembled soldiers and knights, often holding a sacred relic. He would offer them spiritual guidance, blessings, and absolution, assuring them that their mission was holy. Following this, all the men would unite in prayer, focusing on eternal life and the anticipated divine judgment at the end of the world. They would pray for God's protection, asking to be spared from suffering and death. The priest would touch their heads to conclude the ceremony, and each man would stand up to kiss the holy cross. It was a solemn affair, after which the men emerged ready for battle, forgiven of their sins, and prepared to die for God.

The battle at Ceuta was an anticlimax because many of its defenders had already left. Those who remained were caught off-guard, and by the end of the day, the town was in the hands of the Portuguese. The three days that followed were characterized by pillage and massacre. Ceuta was thoroughly and duly sucked of all anti-Portuguese life, and for the first time, Portugal saw riches for herself.

A Portuguese chronicler once observed that Ceuta attracted merchants as far away as Syria, the Barbary Coast, Ethiopia, and Assyria. According to this account, the trading activity was so vibrant and the wealth so considerable that, in comparison, local dwellings seemed modest and unimpressive. As they looked for gold and riches, the attackers opened bags, spilling cinnamon, pepper, and other spices into the streets to be trodden. They looted booths from many traders and smashed glass, porcelain, and tiles as they grabbed decorated carpets. Eventually, they had enough, and it was time to return home. With his sons, the king returned to Portugal and left 2,500 soldiers. The conflict was over in two weeks.

Unfortunately, Ceuta did not prove as profitable as the Portuguese had hoped. It ended up becoming a financial drain. All the Muslim caravans trading in Ceuta headed to Tangier instead, making it their new trading post. The once-rich and vibrant Ceuta market became poor and insignificant. The Portuguese eventually realized that without Tangier, owning Ceuta was no good. Twenty-two years later, they would try to take Tangier. Nevertheless, in Ceuta, for the first time, they enjoyed immense wealth and developed the idea of reaching more riches by sea. This conquest became the first step in creating an empire. It signaled that the Christians would fight Islam wherever it was. Portugal was primarily interested in converting people to Christianity and wealth acquisition.

The capture of Ceuta by the Portuguese in 1415 marked the beginning of a wave of European overseas expansion with global implications. Portugal maintained control over Ceuta until 1668 when it was formally ceded to Spain. This conquest served as a significant stepping stone for Afonso I, the first Duke of

Bragança, who was an illegitimate son of King John I of Portugal. By the time his father, King John I, died in 1433, Afonso I had won favor with the Portuguese elite. Afonso V ascended to the throne as a young boy after the death of his father, King Duarte of Portugal. A regency was established under Leonor of Aragon and the Duke of Coimbra, who proved unpopular. Afonso I of Bragança soon emerged as a key advisor to the young king. In a gesture of reconciliation and goodwill, the Duke of Coimbra elevated Afonso I to the rank of Duke of Bragança in 1442, solidifying the foundation of the House of Bragança.

Because of Afonso I's success and hard work, his children lived privileged lives and secured successful positions. His first son was prominent in the nobility, having been given Nuno Alvares' prestigious and lucrative title of Count of Ourem. He became a successful diplomat in his own right and represented the king in Basel in 1436 and later in the Council of Florence. In 1451, he was made Marquis of Valencia and joined Leonor of Portugal and her husband on several state trips. In 1458, he took part in the capture of Alcacer-Ceguer. He died two years later, and his father followed suit in 1461.

Afonso I's first-born daughter, Isabel of Bragança, married the Lord of Reguengos de Monsaraz, relinking the royal House of Portugal with the House of Bragança. Her strategic marriage proved successful, producing four children whose descendants would greatly influence the Iberian Peninsula. His last child was his successor—the Duke of Bragança, Fernando I, who continued his societal and military legacy. Fernando I was born in 1403, and Nuno Alvares, his grandfather, gave him the title Count of Arraiolos. He eventually became accomplished in the military, participating in many Portuguese imperial campaigns.

Fernando I would be a famous and influential member of the nobility, but he did not always find himself currying favor with the king. At one point, he openly denounced King Duarte I at a Cortes meeting while they discussed whether to rescue the king's brother from the Moors. However, he became a favorite with both the imperial and royal governments when King Afonso V reigned, making him the governor of Ceuta with the titles Count of Neiva and Marquis of Vila Vicosa. He married the Lady of Cadaval, Joana de Castro, and they had children who grew the influence of the House of Bragança. Six of his nine children reached adulthood and secured their status through marriage or career advancement. However, they faced challenges due to the actions of King John II against them.

Fernando II succeeded Fernando I, his first son, who was initially a popular and bright nobleman, but he conflicted with King John II, and his house collapsed. Fernando's second son, John of Bragança, was by then a constable of Portugal and an accomplished man in the military. His third son, Afonso of Bragança, rose by merit and was ceded Count of Faro. His fourth son, Alvaro of Bragança, inherited the fiefs from his mother, which made him the Lord of Ferreira, Cadaval, and Tentugal. Fernando I had only one surviving daughter, Beatriz of Bragança, who married the first Marquis of Vila Real. His last child married Henrique de Meneses, who became the Count of Viana do Antelejo. In the end, all his children and grandchildren suffered under the reign of John II.

During the reign of Fernando II, the House of Bragança had become one of the most prominent noble families in Portugal and was rapidly gaining influence across the Iberian Peninsula. Fernando II expanded the family's legacy by obtaining additional titles, including that of the Duke of Guimaraes. However, King John II aimed to weaken the House of Bragança and the duke as he sought to consolidate power and reduce the influence of the nobility. To achieve his goal, King John II executed numerous nobles from prominent Portuguese families, seized their estates, and forced their families into exile. Fernando II, a significant and influential noble, was accused of treason. He was eventually executed, and his assets and titles were absorbed into the royal holdings. His family members were sent into exile in Castile.

Following the hardships endured due to their father Fernando II's misfortunes, his children faced a difficult childhood. However, King Manuel I, who succeeded John II, pardoned the House of Bragança. He restored their confiscated properties on the condition that they pledge their loyalty to him. Jaime I, Fernando II's eldest surviving son, returned to Portugal. His only other surviving brother, Dinis of Bragança, married the Countess of Lemos, and they had four children.

As the Duke of Bragança, Jaime I's focused on restoring the family's grandeur and reclaiming their place in Portugal after returning from exile. He regained some of the properties previously confiscated from his family. To re-establish the house's prestige, he commissioned the construction of the Palace of Vila Vicosa, which would become one of the grandest palaces in the Iberian Peninsula. Jaime I also worked diligently to become a trusted confidant of King Manuel I and, for a brief period, even stood as his heir apparent. However, Jaime I's tenure was not without controversy. He financed the conquest of Azamor on behalf of the Portuguese crown, an endeavor believed to have been assigned to him as punishment for ordering the murder of his first wife, Leonor Perez.

Jaime I's children, two born by Leonor Perez and eight later born by his second wife, Joana of Mendoca, went on to live successful lives under the now-restored House of Bragança. His first daughter, Isabel of Bragança, married the Duke of Guimaraes, with whom she had three children. One of her sons, Teodosio I, was instrumental in the Portuguese Renaissance. The other children of Jaime I entered religious orders. His second daughter, Joana of Bragança, married the 3rd Marquis of Elche, while the third one married Francisco de Melo, the Marquis of Ferreira. Jaime I's other son, Constantino of Bragança, married the daughter of the 1st Marquis of Ferreira, but they had no children. He became famous as a great Portuguese administrator, serving under the Indian Viceroy of Portugal and, later, the Captain of Ribeira Grande.

Teodosio I is remembered for embodying the spirit of the Portuguese Renaissance as a scholarly nobleman and patron of the arts. While he maintained the prestige of the House of Bragança, he did not leave as significant a mark on its history as some other members did. His first son, who would have been Teodosio II had he lived, died before he could inherit his father's titles, falling in battle at Alcacer Quibir alongside King Sebastian I of Portugal. His daughter married into nobility, becoming the spouse of the first Duke of Caminha.

John I of Bragança, the last child of Teodosio I, had a reign markedly different from that of his scholarly and peaceful father. John I's tenure was tumultuous, most notably marked by the 1580 Portuguese succession crisis. He married Infanta Catarina, the daughter of the Duke of Guimaraes and the granddaughter of King Manuel I. While both were among the candidates for the Portuguese throne, their Habsburg cousin, Philip II of Spain (Philip I of Portugal), ultimately secured the crown, forming the Iberian Union. To placate the House of Bragança, Philip II restored the title of Portuguese constable John I had previously held. He received various other prestigious titles and lands as part of this reconciliation effort.

John I's daughters were some of the most eligible ladies in Iberia, but only one married. His eldest son took part in the battle of Alcacer Quibir at the age of ten and would become a well-respected general. Duarte de Bragança, his second son, became the first Marquis of Frenchila, and his third son earned the title of Archbishop of Evora—both choosing to support Philip I when the monarch tried to influence the House of Bragança. By 1640, it had amassed nearly 80,000 vassals and had patronage over numerous institutions, churches, and orders.

By then, Philip I's policies of respect for Portugal were long past. As mentioned, the country was overtaxed, and Portuguese colonies had no protection. Philip III showed that he had no respect for the Portuguese nobility. According to court historians, when John II became king, he established himself as a modest man without ambitions for the crown. His wife urged him to accept the offer, claiming she preferred to be a queen rather than a duchess. He became John IV of Portugal. The Braganças were finally on the throne. Under his sons, Pedro II and Afonso VI, part of what Portugal had lost during the Iberian Union was restored and expanded, bequeathing new wealth to Portugal.

The zenith of the House of Bragança came with the extended reign of John V, who ruled with righteousness and grandeur between 1706 and 1750. However, a devastating earthquake struck Lisbon in 1755 when his son was king, destabilizing his legacy.

Between 1701 and 1714, Spain was caught in the turmoil of the War of the Spanish Succession. Initially, Portugal sided with the Bourbon claimant to the Spanish throne, a candidate backed by France. The Bourbon family is a European royal house of French origin, and at the time, it was highly influential in

France. Its members had ruled in France, Spain, and other European countries, and a Bourbon monarch on the Spanish throne would significantly strengthen France's position in Europe. Therefore, this alignment initially put Portugal in alliance with France, but the dynamics would shift as the war progressed. However, Portugal later switched sides to join a coalition with Austria, Great Britain, and other nations, opposing France and its allies. Portuguese and Spanish forces fought along their mutual border for several years. At one point, the Anglo-Portuguese alliance even advanced as far as Madrid. Ultimately, the war led to territorial gains for Portugal in Brazil.

For context, it is essential to emphasize the growing instability in Europe at the time. King Charles II of Spain was ill and childless, so European leaders started laying succession claims to take over after him as king of Spain. King Louis XIV of France wanted his eldest son to take over, citing that he was the grandson of King Philip IV. However, the Netherlands and England did not want unity between Spain and France. When Charles II died, he named the Duke of Anjou, Philip, his heir. Philip was also the grandson of Louis XIV.

Concerned about the growing power of France and the potential implications if France gained control over Spanish territories in the Netherlands, several

European powers took action. The Dutch Republic, England, and some German states allied with the Holy Roman Empire to counter the French threat. Their goal was to prevent the Bourbon family from taking the Spanish throne and to seize some Spanish territories in Italy and the Netherlands. Thus, in 1702, the War of the Spanish Succession began.

The War of the Spanish Succession lasted from 1701 to 1714 and had a global impact, including in the American colonies, where it was known as Queen Anne's War. William III of England was succeeded by his sister-in-law, Queen Anne, who was the daughter of James II. The conflict continued for much of Queen Anne's reign. In the Americas, the war primarily featured French privateers operating in the Atlantic and raids conducted by Native American and French forces against English settlements on the frontier. One particularly devastating raid took place in 1704 in Deerfield, Massachusetts. During this attack, Native American and French forces killed fifty-six people, including women and children, and took additional captives back to Canada.

Three years after the devastating raid on Deerfield, colonial forces from Rhode Island, Massachusetts, and other British colonial territories attempted to capture Port Royal, a significant French stronghold in Acadia, present-day Nova Scotia. Their efforts were unsuccessful. However, in 1710, a British fleet led by Francis Nicholson successfully captured the city. Following its capture, Port Royal was renamed Nova Scotia. The War of the Spanish Succession officially ended in 1713 with the Treaty of Utrecht, although this agreement did not fully resolve all the tensions between France, Spain, and Portugal.

7

CONFLICT, NATURAL DISASTER, AND THE AGE OF POMBAL (1740–1777 AD)

From the end of the War of the Spanish Succession until 1750, Portugal was ruled by King John V, who was best known for his lavish lifestyle. His reign saw Portugal's monarchy rise to new levels of prosperity, prestige, and wealth among European courts. It saw a large influx of gold into the royal treasury coffers. This gold mainly came from the "royal fifth," a tax requiring that one-fifth of all precious metals and gems found in colonies go to the Portuguese royal treasury, collected from Maranhão and Brazil, which were still Portuguese colonies. The king spent lavishly on ambitious architectural projects, the most notable of which was Mafra Palace, a grand baroque complex with a palace, monastery, and library near Lisbon. He also diverted much of Portugal's resources toward commissions and his literary and art collections.

In addition, John V had a sizable appetite for international diplomatic recognition. He spent large sums of money building embassies and sending courts to Europe, the most renowned in Rome in 1716 and Paris in 1715. He disregarded traditional Portuguese governance institutions like the Cortes and ruled as an absolute monarch. The gold and diamonds from Brazil financed his way of life and substantially increased the crown's power. Although John tried to restore the navy and stimulate industry, his administration was not eager to rally behind him.

They detested that John V was copying the magnificence of neighboring European courts. They also despised his growing wealth. Even so, John endowed libraries in the country, encouraged scholarships, became a patron of the arts, and in 1720, founded the Royal Academy of History and other architecture and natural history museums. Most of his efforts were geared toward achieving status, but he also gave his energy to a lengthy dispute with the papacy. In his final years, he suffered from ill health, and during that period, his government was dominated by churchmen who were incompetent and neglected the affairs of the country. By that point, John's court was a replica of the

Versailles of Louis XV of France and was filled with his favorite people and mistresses.

Joseph I succeeded his father, John V, and reigned from 1750 to 1777. While he was the nominal ruler, the true power behind the throne was Sebastião José de Carvalho e Melo, or just Carvalho, better known as the Marquis of Pombal. Pombal was a controversial figure —often viewed as a despotic yet innovative statesman. Unlike the relatively uneventful and prosperous period under John V, Joseph I's reign was marked by more active governance, primarily influenced by Pombal. Joseph I seemed content to delegate significant responsibilities to his ministers, allowing him more time to indulge in his personal interests like hunting and opera.

When he was first appointed, Carvalho had not yet earned the title of Marquis of Pombal. His main job was to assist Joseph I in governance. Pombal's policies were aligned with regalism, aiming to consolidate royal authority while diminishing the power of the church and nobility. This created tensions between these traditional pillars of Portuguese society.

In 1758, an assassination attempt on Joseph I provided Carvalho an opportunity to crack down on several noble families. A year later, in 1759, he expelled the Jesuits, mainly because he viewed them as a threat to royal authority and an obstacle to his efforts to modernize Portugal. All the while, Joseph unquestioningly and unconditionally accepted Carvalho's version of events. In 1775, the statue of Joseph I was inaugurated, which still stands in the Praça do Comércio (formerly known as Terreiro do Paço) in Lisbon. By this time, Carvalho had become the Marquis of Pombal, a title he was granted in 1769 in recognition of his service to the crown. Pombal seized the inauguration as an opportunity to showcase the reforms he had implemented in Portugal's armed forces, finances, administration, and education. His rise to power and influence was catalyzed by his decisive actions following the devastating Lisbon earthquake of 1755, which laid the groundwork for his comprehensive efforts to rebuild and modernize the country.

That fateful day of the earthquake had started like any other day in Lisbon—parishioners were out for mass, and servants were busy preparing meals and holiday feasts. Approximately 300 kilometers from this activity in Lisbon, deep on the ocean floor, the tectonic plates of America, Eurasia, and Africa were meeting at a geological hotspot. The Atlantic Ocean, up until then, had been seismically quiet, but that morning, the plates slipped and released the energy of 32,000 Hiroshima bombs. The waves and tremors rippled across the North Atlantic, causing rivers in Scotland to rise and claiming lives as far away as Brazil. Lisbon endured a catastrophic disaster.

At around 9 a.m., the tremors rumbled underneath the city, ringing the city's bells in unison like a warning sign. Later, when recounting the day's events, survivors would remember the horrible noise from the bells just before the ground started shaking. In six minutes, cathedrals had crumpled, and whole neighborhoods were buried. Within an hour, a six-meter-high tsunami struck the waterfront, claiming the lives of hundreds who had sought safety there. Concurrently, numerous small fires, ignited by votive candles and cooking hearths, began to merge into a massive firestorm. This blaze continued for five days, ultimately reducing what remained of Lisbon to ruins.

The Lisbon earthquake initiated a paradoxical chapter in Portugal's relationship with its capital city. While the disaster wrought immense devastation, it also paved the way for significant reforms and the modernization of Lisbon. For the years leading to the disaster, the monarchy had grown fat on the bounty from her maritime empire that had penetrated India and Brazil. The seafaring Portuguese had made a name for them-selves all over the world. Yet, seafaring was not held highly in society then. Very few colonial spoils were reinvested into the citizenry beyond the nobility. In one day, the ocean leveled Lisbon, the nexus of the empire, where most of its wealth was stored in massive warehouses on the waterfront. One warehouse destroyed was the Casa de India, estimated to have had 1.5% of Portugal's GDP in diamonds from Brazil.

Not long after the 8.5 earthquake obliterated Lisbon, Pombal mounted a stallion, galloped through the ruins, and reached Joseph I. At the time, the monarch had just escaped death by staying at his country palace rather than the city. As someone who valued philandering and hunting more than governing, the king did not know how to restore his kingdom, so in a moment that would define Portugal's history, he gave Pombal the authority to do what he couldn't. Sensing the king's uncertainty, Pombal started ordering his aides and, in no time, had commandeered the country's recovery efforts. After the earthquake, Joseph I developed severe claustrophobia and chose to reside in a luxurious tent for the remainder of his life. While he remained the nominal king, the real governance was effectively carried out by Pombal.

The devout Catholic population in Lisbon thought of the event as divine punishment. Similarly, the Protestant European countries thought the destruction was God's judgment on Portugal for backward Catholic beliefs. To Pombal, the event created a path to power and a chance to rewrite the future of a colonial state that had been crumbling. Pombal gathered a team of military engineers and imposed a design over the medieval streets of the Baixa neighborhood in Lisbon. The result was today's orderly and elegant city. It was designed to speed up evacuation in emergencies in the future and improve sewage, transportation, and garbage collection.

For the next twenty-two years that Pombal was in power, he would become controversial for using Lisbon's destruction to force the country with strong religious ties into its modern era. The Lisbon that arose following the earthquake differed from the Lisbon that went down. The redesigned city incorporated advanced ideas in disaster preparedness, architecture, and seismology. These innovations continue to benefit the people of Portugal today, especially in preparing for future natural disasters like tsunamis.

Approximately two-thirds of Lisbon's diverse housing stock was decimated in the earthquake. The new Pombal decree mandated that buildings have firewalls and wooden frames that swayed with seismic forces. Pombal's engineers designed the wooden-framed "Pombalina cage" to withstand small to medium earthquakes. If the shaking is extreme, the façade of the building may collapse, but most of its structure would remain intact. Pombal also conducted other futuristic efforts, including building drains under city streets to counteract flooding. He instructed workers to install timber pilings under the city's sandy soil to ensure the foundations of the buildings were secure. They also built a foreshore along the River Tagus because the river flows through the city and into its harbor.

The new Lisbon was taking shape on top of the old one. Recently, during the construction of the subway in the city, a team of archeologists discovered that the ruins of the earthquake spread up to 15 meters deep. The demolished buildings raised the city's foundations above the waterline, insulating Lisbon from future tsunamis. Today, the world over, Pombal's innovations are recognized as the earliest efforts at integrating disaster planning into urban design.

Before that earthquake, Pombal had spent much of his time in Austria and England, interacting with enlightenment ideas while the aristocracy and the church ruled Portugal using brute medieval force. When Pombal was put in charge, he took after the enlightened tyrants of his time—emulating leaders like Catherine the Great, who used their power to impose reform. However, Pombal had a brutal streak that would flash anytime the aristocracy or the church tried to regain control. In one example of a ruthless retaliation, he learned of a foiled plot to take the king's life. He rounded up the most powerful families in Portugal to interrogate and torture them.

After the interrogation, Pombal publicly executed some members of the Tavora family who were accused of the plot. He banned the Tavora name and renamed a river by the same name to the River of Death. He was known for excessive use of force when he deemed it necessary. This played a role in his unpopularity in high and low society. When Joseph I died, Pombal was ousted immediately and banished by the king's daughter. He still had two decades to institute innovative reforms, which we can see and study today.

Several geophysicists rely on Pombal's work today. One is Maria Ana Baptista, who wrote a doctoral dissertation modeling the tsunami using historical poems, letters, scientific observations, and sermons written at the time. Most of her data was drawn from a survey that Pombal sent to every parish in Portugal just after the earthquake. The questionnaire was striking because it did not mention God at all. Pombal was only interested in factual observations like when the earthquake started, the length of the shaking, and whether people saw any abnormalities at sea or along springs and rivers. He collected 646 responses.

Other scholars describe the 1755 earthquake as Europe's first modern disaster—a name that attracts the attention of many seismologists. They agree that a similar transoceanic tsunami and earthquake is unlikely to strike Lisbon again. Other tsunami disasters that have hit Lisbon have not been as powerful. In the Baixa district that Pombal rebuilt, the lessons of the earthquake are fading among the residents today. Not many Portuguese live in the neighborhood. It has become gentrified, accommodating many tourists and foreign workers. It is suspected that the current inhabitants would still make the same mistake made in 1755 by running for refuge toward the riverfront.

The original building facades remain, but the owners are now allowed to change the structure of the Pombalina cage inside, which jeopardizes its integrity. As the city has grown, the riverfront has grown with it. The earthquake caused the previously unstable land at the riverfront to transform into a liquefied mud-like terrain. Portugal may need to do more to improve disaster preparedness. Even so, Pombal started a significant tradition of using science to safeguard Lisbon. Because of that, he is tied to the past and Portugal's future. Joseph I died in 1777, ending Pombal's power, and the church and the nobles recovered their supremacy.

8

A HUNDRED YEARS OF STRIFE, OVERTHROWING THE MONARCHY, AND DECLARING THE FIRST REPUBLIC (1778–1926 AD)

While Pombal revolutionized many aspects of Portugal's economy, other countries like Spain were making global moves. In 1762, the Spaniards invaded Portugal in one of the most challenging situations King Joseph I faced beyond the earthquake. The Spanish were trying to conquer Portugal as one of their military episodes of the Seven Years' War. Some historians consider this to be the first true World War. It was led by two of the greatest rivals in Europe—France and Britain. The British decided to help the Portuguese during the invasion, while the French supported Spain.

Earlier, France and Spain gave King Joseph I an ultimatum to either abandon his alliance with Britain and close any ports to British ships or deal with an invasion as Britain had become too powerful. The monarch, advised by Pombal, refused to submit and started preparing for war. Immediately, Britain deployed 7,100 troops to provide relief. More significantly, they sent a military commander, the Count of Lippe, to help lead the defense. The Count instituted reforms in the military and offered training to the Portuguese army, playing a pivotal role in leading the alliance to victory.

This period saw the unfolding of the French Revolution, a tumultuous event that shook the European political landscape. During the revolution's early years, Spain's King Charles IV initially sympathized with the French monarchy, led by his Bourbon relative, King Louis XVI of France. However, after Louis XVI was executed in 1793, Spain joined the First Coalition against Revolutionary France. Despite some early setbacks, the French army eventually gained the upper hand over various opposing forces. In 1795, Spain withdrew from the coalition against France.

For the subsequent decade, Charles IV's reign was characterized by an ineffective and corrupt government, heavily influenced by Manuel Godoy, the queen's favorite and purported lover. This period saw Spain aligning more closely with Revolutionary and Napoleonic France in several military conflicts. Ultimately, the Spanish fleet, in alliance with the

French, suffered a decisive defeat at the hands of Admiral Nelson at the Battle of Trafalgar in 1805.

Napoleon Bonaparte gradually gained influence over Manuel Godoy and King Charles IV of Spain. At the same time, Ferdinand, Charles' son and heir to the Spanish throne, led opposition against Godoy and his father. Despite his character flaws, Ferdinand was viewed by many in Spain as a national hero. Napoleon initially saw his influence over Spanish leaders as a stepping stone to effectively taking control of Spain. In 1807, Napoleon compelled Spain to join forces with him in invading Portugal, a country that continued to allow British ships into its ports. This action breached Napoleon's "Continental System," a blockade to prevent British trade with European nations. Napoleon's ultimate goal was to cripple British trade and force Britain into submission.

Expectedly, Portugal was overrun very quickly. In one month, Lisbon was taken by Marshal Junot from France, and the royal family fled to Brazil. With his armies securely positioned in Spain, Napoleon forced both Ferdinand and Charles to abdicate their claims to the Spanish throne. He installed his brother Joseph as the new King of Spain in their place. Meanwhile, Ferdinand and Charles were given estates and pensions in France, where they stayed detained. However,

Napoleon did not account for the feelings of the Spanish and Portuguese people. They were devoted to their religion, national pride, and kings, so they rose instinctively against him.

The populace did not have organized armies, and their plans were not cohesive. For example, the province of Asturias declared war against France, but guerilla bands and irregular forces proved difficult to subdue. French armies constantly harassed them. In 1808, Britain dispatched an army under Sir Arthur Wellesley (before he became the Duke of Wellington) to Portugal. He was supposed to station there and help drive the French away after defeating them at Vimeiro, a town in the Lisbon District of western Portugal. Before this event could occur, Spanish guerrilla fighters scored a significant victory over the French at the Battle of Bailén, resulting in the surrender of 18,000 French soldiers. Following the battle at Vimeiro in the Lisbon District of western Portugal, Wellesley was recalled to England.

Napoleon personally led an invasion of Spain to stabilize the situation in France's favor. He assembled a sizable army and successfully occupied Madrid. To halt his further advances southwards, the British government dispatched an expeditionary force led by Sir John Moore, entering Spain from Portugal. This maneuver forced Napoleon and his marshals to divert their focus to address this new threat. They successfully pushed the British forces to evacuate Spain via the port of Corunna in 1809. After the British evacuation, Wellesley was sent back to the Iberian Peninsula with reinforcements to protect Portugal. On this occasion, he was successful, notably through his victory at the Battle of Oporto.

However, during the winter of 1811, Wellesley had to fall back and strengthen his defensive positions around the Lines of Torres Vedras in Portugal. Later that same year, Wellesley took command of a joint British and Portuguese force to engage in the Peninsular War. In Portugal, this conflict is also known as the War of Independence. Wellington supported Spanish guerrilla activities across the peninsula to keep French forces occupied. General Rowland Hill, a British army officer serving under Wellington, was assigned the mission of disrupting communications between Napoleon's marshals. This strategic move led to the isolation of Marshal Marmont, Wellington's primary adversary at the time. In June, Wellington advanced to Salamanca in western Spain, where he successfully captured three forts within ten days, pressuring Marmont's forces to take action.

Marmont hesitated to engage directly, leading Wellington to initiate maneuvers to gain a tactical advantage and force a battle. Wellington received intelligence reports suggesting that additional troops were being sent by Joseph Bonaparte, making him consider a withdrawal from Salamanca back to Portugal. Despite these concerns, it should be noted that Wellington had already achieved significant victories in the Peninsular War, including the Battle of Talavera, which had earned him the title of Viscount Wellington. At Salamanca, he commanded a robust force of 48,000 Spanish and Portuguese troops and 60 artillery pieces.

In July 1812, skirmishes broke out in the hills of Salamanca. The two armies, Marmont's and Wellington's, kept moving southwest. Marmont tried to block Wellington from returning to Portugal, but his forces stayed hidden along the northeast ridges. Marmont made the mistake of assuming that he knew his enemy. Wellington was a general who tended to be defensive. He would not be attacked on a ground that he did not choose. So, when Marmont noticed dusty clouds created by Wellington's baggage train, he assumed the whole army was retreating. He ordered his army to divide into three and cut off Wellington. That would be his undoing.

Wellington seized the opportunity. He realized that Marmont's forces were now overstretched, so he launched a series of blows against the French. Soon enough, they were shattered. Marmont and his second-in-command were wounded early in the battle, leaving General Bertrand to take over command. Bertrand then attempted to breach Wellington's central defenses. Against a less experienced commander, this could have saved the French army, but Wellington was more experienced. He brought reinforcements to shore up his defenses, and by the end of the day, only one division in the French army remained intact. The rest had been devastated.

That day, Marmont's army lost over 14,000 men and 20 artillery pieces, while his opponent lost half as many men. The defeat would have been worse if the Spanish garrison had not abandoned their station at the river crossing, which allowed the French to escape. The Battle of Salamanca proved that Wellington could maneuver and win in the open field, but he lost his reputation as a defensive general. The victory gave the British a psychological high that would power them for the rest of the war. Later on, Wellington was able to save Madrid. With Joseph Bonaparte's authority undermined in Spain, French garrisons were weakening.

Moreover, the victory persuaded the British that pursuing the war in the north was worth it. It proved that Napoleon could be defeated. Following the battle, Wellington succeeded in liberating southern Spain from enemy control. In 1813, Wellington secured a decisive victory at Vittoria, a town in northern Spain near the Basque Country. By the end of that year, his forces had successfully pushed the French back across the border in the Battle of the Pyrenees. As Wellington advanced into southern France, the widespread collapse of French resistance on multiple fronts led Napoleon to surrender. The Spanish and Portuguese insurrections played an essential role in Napoleon's defeat. Their initial uprisings against a dominant France served as a catalyst, inspiring similar revolts in other countries that followed.

Not only that, but they provided a base for British operations in the Peninsula, which helped to hold down French forces and prevented their use in Napoleon's other wars. Though their military methods lacked a clear plan, at times only keeping alive due to Wellington's patience, their guerrillas significantly contributed to the success of Wellington's campaigns.

During the war, the Cortes had been elected and established in the city of Cádiz. At the time, Cádiz was one of the few areas in Spain not under French control. The Cortes was convened in the name of King Ferdinand VII. In 1812, this assembly promulgated a liberal constitution that included provisions for universal male suffrage and other democratic principles. This marked a significant departure from the political landscape in Portugal before the war.

After the war, Ferdinand VII ascended to the Spanish throne and initially pledged to uphold the liberal Constitution of 1812—a promise he promptly reneged on. Capitalizing on his popularity, he discarded the constitution and purged its liberal proponents. Some were exiled, others executed, and still others imprisoned. Ferdinand reinstated absolute monarchy, but his ineffective rule fueled widespread dissatisfaction. In 1820, Colonel Rafael del Riego led a revolt that compelled him to reinstate the 1812 constitution. Ferdinand subsequently sought the aid of European powers, aligning himself with Prussia and Russia to quash liberal movements. This "Holy Alliance" agreed to bypass any British objections and even plotted to restore the Bourbon monarchy in France.

In 1823, a French army invaded Spain with the aim of ousting the liberals and reinstating Ferdinand VII's absolute rule. The invasion encountered little resistance, as the general populace was not yet ready to embrace liberal reforms. Meanwhile, in Portugal, a British-led regency had governed the country during the war, given that King John VI had been absent. Wary of the rise of liberalism, John VI made no immediate plans to return to Portugal even after the conflicts had subsided. The example set by Spain's liberal Constitution of 1812, coupled with the absence of the royal family in Portugal, fueled discontent and unrest among the Portuguese. This eventually led to a liberal revolution in 1820, which resulted in the establishment of a democratic constitution.

In 1822, King John VI was persuaded to return to Portugal to reign as a constitutional monarch. However, in 1824, his second son, Miguel, led an unsuccessful attempt to overturn the democratic constitution. When John VI returned to Portugal, the Portuguese Cortes opted to grant Brazil a status of dependency. This decision stoked nationalist sentiments in Brazil, a territory that by then had a larger population than Portugal and had served as the seat of the royal family for over a decade. Pedro, John VI's son, who had been left in Brazil as Prince Regent, chose to remain there despite efforts by the Portuguese government to recall him. He eventually declared Brazil's independence and assumed the title of Emperor.

By the end of that year, the Portuguese garrisons in Brazil were largely defeated, thanks in significant part to the efforts of the Brazilian navy, commanded by Lord Cochrane, a British naval officer renowned for his daring exploits. With that, three centuries of Portuguese rule in Brazil ended. This rule was characterized by the tyranny of the church and slave labor, but with some infrequent exceptions, the area enjoyed the advantage of peace. As a lasting legacy, Portuguese and Spanish were left as the major languages, and Roman Catholicism remained the predominant religion. Brazil inherited the knowledge necessary for future innovations in industry, agriculture, irrigation, road building, and commerce.

In numerous respects, Portugal during the 19th century bore a striking resemblance to Spain in the same era, as both countries experienced periods marked by internal discord and turmoil. After returning to Portugal, King John VI died in 1826. Pedro, already the Emperor of Brazil, inherited the Portuguese throne from his father, King John VI. However, Pedro chose to remain in Brazil and abdicated the Portuguese throne in favor of his infant daughter, Maria. His brother Miguel was appointed as regent for the young queen. Initially, the plan was for Maria to marry Miguel eventually, and they would jointly rule under a constitutional charter. Although Miguel initially accepted this arrangement, his mother's influence led him to settle old scores and declare himself the sole king of Portugal. While countries like Spain, Russia, and the United States recognized Miguel's claim to the throne, liberal factions within Portugal did not accept his rule.

In 1830, as the Duke of Wellington considered recognizing Miguel as the legitimate king of Portugal, the situation changed dramatically. Pedro I of Brazil, Maria's father, abdicated the Brazilian throne in favor of his son, Pedro II, and returned to Europe to support his daughter Maria's claim to the Portuguese throne. This led to six years of civil war in Portugal. Miguel was eventually deposed in 1834, allowing Maria to assume the throne, where she ruled until 1853 amidst ongoing political turmoil. Maria was a member of the House of Bragança, being the daughter of Pedro I and his first wife. After Maria's death, her son Pedro V succeeded her and ruled from 1853 to 1861, followed by his brother Louis, who reigned until 1889.

During the reigns of brothers Pedro V and Louis I, Portugal experienced a relative decrease in civil unrest. The nation oscillated between liberal and conservative governments, a pattern also observed in neighboring Spain. However, republican sentiments began to rise, culminating in the formation of a Republican Party in 1881.

The Republican Party in Portugal began positioning itself as a force that could bring positive changes to the nation. Public support for the monarchy was waning, a situation the 1890 British Ultimatum worsened. The ultimatum forced Portugal to abandon its ambitious

Pink Map project, which sought to claim sovereignty over the land corridor between its colonies of Mozambique and Angola. The rapid capitulation of the Portuguese government was perceived as a humiliation by both the general population and the country's elite. Further exacerbating the situation, King Carlos I's intervention in the country's financial affairs worsened an already existing financial crisis.

As the Republican Party gained traction, it saw increasing electoral success, particularly in 1890. This rise in popularity signaled growing public disapproval of the monarchy. Despite internal divisions over ideology and political strategy, party members were unified in their objective to end monarchical rule. The Republican Party also distinguished itself from the Socialist Party, which focused primarily on advocating for workers' rights.

The Republican Party was committed to establishing a democratic system in Portugal, with key support from Teofilo Braga, a prominent writer, scholar, and later Provisional President of the Portuguese First Republic. This democratic focus attracted support from segments of the bourgeoisie. In a related development, Antonio Jose de Almeida, who was studying at Coimbra University, published an article criticizing the king. This led to his imprisonment, although he would later become the President of the Portuguese Republic.

Louis I was succeeded by his son, Carlos I, who was known for his extravagant lifestyle. This period was marked by increasing public dissatisfaction and licentiousness. In 1906, Carlos I dissolved the parliamentary government to suppress growing opposition.

Tragically, in 1908, both he and his crown prince were assassinated by anarchists. While traveling from Alentejo to Lisbon, the king and his heir were killed. They were traveling on an open carriage, and as they greeted the crowd at the commerce square, a group of men shot them many times. Two of the attackers were killed, but the others escaped. Portugal was left with no king. Manuel II, the second son of Carlos I, ascended to the throne and reinstated the constitutional government. However, a revolution in 1910 led to his forced abdication and exile from the country.

In October 1910, the Republican uprising started in Lisbon. Initially, many Republicans were not interested in participating in the rebellion, but eventually, there were enough for it to succeed. Nearly 2,000 armed sailors and soldiers showed up.

The local government had anticipated assistance from military units stationed in other regions, but that help never materialized. Rebel forces effectively disrupted military communications by cutting off communication lines and isolating Lisbon, preventing orders from being received. They also sabotaged railway tracks to delay the arrival of troops from outside the capital. Although there was a possibility that military support could come from Setubal, the rebels took control of the Tagus River, further hindering reinforcements. Outmaneuvered, the military had no choice but to acknowledge the collapse of the monarchy and the establishment of a republic. The revolution was not without violence; shootings and bombings occurred, though the exact number of casualties remains unknown.

Portugal was then declared a republic, a status it has maintained today. Although the Portuguese republic outlasted Spain's two republican ventures, it faced challenges in its early years. The revolution was notable for effectively ending the dwindling power of the Portuguese monarchy, which had been further weakened by public dissatisfaction following the assassination of King Carlos I. The revolution represented a desire among the Portuguese people to modernize their country and align it with evolving views on governance, as monarchies were increasingly seen as outdated institutions.

After Portugal was proclaimed a republic, members of the Republican Party created a provisional government that would govern Portugal until a new constitution was approved. Teofilo Braga led the government as president, and seven other men headed the ministries for justice, treasury, internal affairs, war, navy, foreign relations, and public works. The government took steps to set it apart from the former government under the monarchy. They made deals with people who had been victims of the monarchy and forgave everyone who had been prosecuted for crimes against religion or the state. They also closed convents and prohibited religious lessons in schools, choosing secularization instead.

Divorce became permissible, and equality of marriage rights for women and men was promoted. The Catholic Church lost its power over the government, which it did not take well. The provisional government also changed press laws to reduce censorship. They got rid of royal and noble titles. Workers were given the right to strike, a significant step toward labor rights. Portuguese colonies overseas stayed colonized, but they were given more autonomy. Perhaps the most significant change was the adoption of new national symbols. The national flag and anthem were changed, and the escudo was adopted as the new currency.

The provisional government remained in power until February 1911, when the Constituent Assembly was convened. By April of the same year, the Political Constitution of the Portuguese Republic was ratified. Manuel de Arriaga became the first elected constitutional president of the Republic. Ten months after the Constituent Assembly first gathered, the provisional government stepped down, marking the official start of the First Portuguese Republic. This period lasted sixteen years and saw eight different presidents, representing a significant shift in Portuguese history. It bridged the gap between the previous monarchical system and the authoritarian Estado Novo regime that would follow. The First Portuguese Republic ended in 1926 with a coup d'état, which ushered in a period of national dictatorship that eventually led to the establishment of the Estado Novo in 1933.

The First Portuguese Republic, which lasted from 1910 to 1926, made some progress toward establishing democracy but faced significant challenges. While it took steps like separating church and state and secularizing education, it failed to quash ongoing royalist plots. Public unrest persisted, fueled by idealists and discontent among the lower classes, who saw slight material improvement in their lives despite the revolution. The period was marked by political instability, featuring numerous insurrections and coups.

Additionally, the country grappled with administrative inefficiency, corruption, and worsening financial conditions. A high illiteracy rate of 65% also posed challenges to the effective implementation of democratic governance.

The situation was so dire that, in 1920 alone, Portugal had nine governments. Amid this chaos, the country was drawn into the First World War against Germany. Its troops were fighting on the Western Front of France and in East Africa. The regime was overthrown in 1926 by an army revolt following a counter-insurrection that was defeated. In 1928, General Carmona became the president of Portugal. He appointed Dr. Salazar, a professor of economics at Coimbra University, as prime minister. In an impressively short time, he was able to balance the budget. For the next forty years, Salazar, an intellectual, retiring man, would become the virtual dictator of Portugal while Carmona was president.

9

PORTUGAL UNDER SALAZAR AND OTHER MILITARY DICTATORS (1933–1974 AD)

Antonio de Oliveira Salazar stands out among modern dictators for his reserved and ascetic personality, in contrast to the more flamboyant and demagogic styles of contemporaries like Adolf Hitler, Benito Mussolini, and Francisco Franco. Despite his unassuming demeanor, Salazar held power in Portugal for four decades, a feat unmatched by those other dictators. He maintained his grip on power by aligning himself with conservative forces, including wealthy landowners, industrialists, and bankers. Salazar allocated a significant portion of the national budget—up to 40%—to the armed forces while exerting control over the media and trade unions. His policies kept the Portuguese economy relatively stable. Still, they left most of the country's nine million citizens in a state of illiteracy and poverty, conditions that helped sustain his long rule.

During Salazar's tenure, Portugal had the lowest per capita income in Europe, at $420, and the region's highest illiteracy rate. In a period marked by global political and social change, Salazar was steadfast in resisting such shifts within Portugal and its colonies. At that time, the colonies—including Mozambique and Angola—had a combined population of thirteen million. Despite the rise of nationalist movements in these territories, Salazar kept them closely tied to Portugal for most of his time in power. In 1968, he deployed 100,000 troops to these colonies to maintain colonial authority. Additionally, as of 1961, all Africans living in Portuguese territories were granted Portuguese citizenship.

Salazar was a quiet autocrat who avoided any personal appeal to popular passions but was very open about his totalitarian beliefs. He was often quoted as saying that the Portuguese needed to be treated like children—if you give them too much too often, you spoil them. He thought of himself as anti-parliamentarian—he said, "I hate the verbosity of the speeches, the meaningless interpolations and the flowery language, the way we waste passion and that not on a great idea, but around futile nothingness from the perspective of the national good." He constantly compared himself with Mussolini, saying that their dictatorships were similar in that they strengthened authority and waged war against some democratic principles. They had a nationalist character mainly grounded on social order. He also acknowledged that he was different in how he discharged his authority.

Salazar's personal life was also austere. He preferred working with the Roman Catholic Church, whose attitudes and moralities he shared. At least on the surface, Portugal under Salazar appeared straitlaced and remarkably staid. Perhaps it was influenced by the dictator's personal life punctuated by mass attendance and daily prayers. Some of his people followed his example. Frequently, he stated that his regime was based on the values necessary to defend, including family, work, authority, country, and God.

To him, education was the family's responsibility. As far as he was concerned, women did their most fruitful work at home. Salazar disapproved of idle men, an attitude that influenced his policies. People who became unemployed got very few insurance benefits and would often be enlisted into public service. He eschewed bread and circuses to win the approval of his people. He was sure that you could not govern the crowds and charm them simultaneously. He did not even give them increasing material prosperity, saying that as far as poverty is concerned, there are no fast solutions. Salazar's economic policies emphasized fiscal conservatism and monetary stability, often prioritizing these over rapid improvements in living standards.

It is said that Salazar liked to quote Machiavelli when prescribing patience and firmness: 'The motto of the wimpy men of our day is to wait for the blessings of time." He also shared Machiavelli's belief that the business of government is too important to leave to the people. According to him, nations' great problems cannot be solved by rank and file. The elite solves them. The masses need only group themselves by these elites. Surprisingly, he won the respect of many different politicians. His fellow fascists admired him, of course, but African supremacist leaders and liberal Britons also admired him. He was praised in the United States among people like Dean Acheson as a remarkable man close to Plato's philosopher king.

In Portugal, however, he was not regarded as enthusiastically. His associates found him to be a solitary man with no interest in close relationships. Often, he would dismiss his ministers with brief notes. He was abrupt when dealing with his subordinates. Once, a minister arrived for an interview without a hat, and after the conversation was over, Salazar rose and placed his own hat on the man's head, saying that ministers look better with hats. His work was his life. He led a frugal and unostentatious lifestyle, abstaining from romantic or marital relationships.

Salazar was a bachelor who lived in a two-story stone house close to the government seat in Lisbon. The house was connected to a church by a passage that he often used when going to pray. Behind the white-washed walls of his house was a pine garden with some flowers and palms. His only known hobby was taking care of those flowers. Besides his housekeeper, Salazar shared his home with Micas and Maria Antonia, his adopted daughters. He stayed occupied with state duties for more than 12 hours every day, even into his late 70s. His office was medium-sized, with walls lined with books and paintings. There was a desk and some leather chairs, with no files or telephone. His things were comfortable, nonofficial, unpretentious, and simple.

Salazar faced opposition, but it was fragmented and ineffective, which bolstered his confidence in his governance. While he was deeply involved in the administrative aspects of ruling the country, he was generally disinterested in engaging in intellectual debates or the social aspects of politics unless absolutely necessary. He was convinced that God was on his side. In 1968, a Western diplomat said many years of repressive tactics had most likely reduced the population to lethargy. The capital, Lisbon, was under his strict rule. It remained orderly, subdued, quiet, and filled with patient and somber people. Perhaps that was something to do with mirroring their leader. In 1960, a reporter wrote that he had a nearly transparent face. Only his black eyes seemed interested and alive. Everything else about him appeared bloodless and faded, from his gray hair to his long and loosely veined hands.

The grayness the reporter observed had appeared in Salazar's character from the beginning. He was born in 1889 in Vimieiro, in northern Portugal, to Maria and Antonio Salazar, innkeepers and peasants. Ambitious for their children, they sent him and his siblings to their literate neighbors to learn until a school opened near them in 1899. A year later, Salazar qualified to be admitted to the Jesuit seminary, where he became his mother's "little priest." He studied there until 1908 and discovered that his true calling was education. In 1910, while the country was approaching the uprising, he entered the University of Coimbra. There, Republicanism was rampant. King Manuel II was deposed as a prelude to introducing the parliamentary system modeled after Britain. It was a period of economic and political confusion, which did not impress Salazar.

To support himself while studying, Salazar worked as a tutor. In 1914, he earned a Bachelor of Arts degree and soon joined the teaching staff. Within four years, he had become an economics professor and received two academic awards. He later earned a doctorate in law. Salazar entered politics when he helped establish the Catholic Center Party, a party guided by the social principles outlined in 19th-century papal encyclicals. In 1921, he became one of the centrists elected to the Cortes. After participating in just one legislative session, Salazar resigned and returned to academia, stating that he found parliamentary debates unproductive.

When the military coup overthrew the government in 1926, the generals asked Salazar, known for his economic prowess by then, to take charge of the Ministry of Finance. He demanded freedom to execute the changes he deemed fit, and when this was refused, he chose to teach. Two years later, General Carmona engineered his election as Portugal's president, giving Salazar power over the country's finances. Immediately after he entered office, Salazar cut public spending and exercised judicious taxation. He balanced the budget within a year, which hadn't happened since 1910. He soon liquidated foreign debt and lifted Portugal's escudo into a premium.

Salazar's accomplishments granted him considerable influence, which he held onto tenaciously. Formalizing his role as a dominant figure, he was appointed Prime Minister in 1932 and retained the position thereafter. He drafted a constitution for a New State (Estado Novo). The constitution was approved in 1933 and proclaimed Portugal a single and corporative state. Practically, though, only one party—Salazar's—was represented at the National Assembly. The president appointed the cabinet, but it was not accountable to the Assembly. Salazar was both Finance Minister and Prime Minister in those early days of the charter. Later, on an interim basis, he was also the Minister of War, Minister for Colonies, and Foreign Minister. His decree initiated worker compensation into law, creating a form of social security, but he also outlawed strikes, making them a crime.

When the Spanish Civil War broke out, Salazar fully supported Generalissimo Francisco Franco, the leader of the Nationalist forces, and officially recognized his government in 1938. During this tumultuous period on the Iberian Peninsula, Salazar established a youth movement akin to Hitler's aimed at preparing young people for military service. He also founded the

Portuguese Legion, tasked with combating internal Communism. These organizations and the army proved instrumental in quelling a popular uprising in Lisbon shortly before the Second World War. Throughout the war, Portugal maintained a position of neutrality, which proved financially beneficial. The country received funds from the United States and Britain to use the Azores Islands as air and naval bases. Lisbon also served as a hub for espionage activities, as Portugal allowed trade with Allied and Axis powers. In the early years of the Cold War, Portugal joined the North Atlantic Treaty Organization (NATO) in 1949 to align with Western powers against the spread of Communism. Only later, in 1955, Portugal became a member of the United Nations.

In Portugal, the war created some pressure for a measure of democracy, so in 1945, Salazar allowed opposition candidates to run for office. The loose coalition that formed at the time, the Movimento Unidade Democratia, was suppressed quickly when it started showing strength in 1948. Salazar outlawed it as a communist front. In 1951, President Carmona died, and Salazar was given an offer for the presidency, which he turned down, claiming that he neither had the physical strength nor the moral ability to begin a new life in a new office. He stayed on as prime minister but acted with less vigor while dealing with nationalism in

Portugal's colonies and the opposition at home. In 1961, nationalist movements in the colonies became openly active. Portugal's colonies at the time included the Cape Verdes Islands, Angola, Portuguese Guinea, Mozambique, Goa, Macao, and Timor.

The enclave of Goa in India had been under Portuguese control for 400 years before it was annexed by India in 1961. While Portugal vehemently protested this action, it ultimately had to accept the situation. Meanwhile, in Africa, Angola—Portugal's largest colony—was experiencing the beginnings of a long-running insurrection. This movement gained international attention in January 1961, when General Humberto Delgado, a Portuguese Air Force officer and former presidential candidate, was indirectly linked to the hijacking of the Portuguese liner Santa Maria in the Caribbean. While Delgado did not directly lead the seizure, the incident was cited as an example of the growing guerrilla activities in Angola. General Delgado would be mysteriously killed a few years later in Spain, but not before the Santa Maria was surrendered after ten days under international pressure.

Salazar responded to this revolt using a double-pronged approach. First, he ordered that the Angolans be bombed into submission, and then he tried to address venality and corruption among their economic exploiters and rulers. He succeeded in containing the revolt for a while, or at least keeping superficial order by force and introducing some reforms. However, the price paid for these actions was heavy, and soon enough, there was a strain on the budget because of military costs. Additionally, at least 1,500 soldiers and officers died during that period. Salazar remained stubborn, though, saying that Portugal had a right to these territories because it discovered them when they were mostly uninhabited.

Towards the end of 1967, the Lisbon government announced that it would not recognize African leadership in any of its colonies, implying that it would not acknowledge the legitimacy of any African leaders there. Salazar believed doing so would lead to instability and a regression to what he considered "backward" African states. Meanwhile, in Portugal, resistance against Salazar's rule had been growing. In 1962, an unsuccessful revolt was followed by several failed coup attempts. Mário Soares, a prominent Portuguese socialist and anti-fascist politician, led the most significant opposition against Salazar's regime. In response, Salazar deployed his security forces against these opposition groups and had Mário Soares deported to the island of São Tomé.

Toward the end of Salazar's life, he still seemed in control despite frequent stirrings and protests. He ignored the critics, convinced he was guiding the country in its best interests. Salazar was sure that most of the world was progressing too fast. He viewed his role in power as a moderating force against excessive change. His dictatorship lasted seven years longer than Franco's in Spain. Throughout that period, he introduced a new constitution, set up the Estado Novo, and prescribed an authoritarian state built on social principles that, to him, made a stable government, modeling it after Mussolini's Italy. He made a provision for a president-appointed cabinet, a chamber representing workers, and a National Assembly, but their only power was advisory.

He may have been modest, but he was still a dictator. His rule shared some aspects with Franco's in that there was only one political party, the press was censored, strikes were made illegal, and any political opponents faced the threat of imprisonment. However, Salazar may have been, in some ways, more ruthless. His regime did nothing to ease the widespread poverty or provide education to the lower classes, who were mostly illiterate. However, it bestowed on Portugal some sense of solvency and stability. There was notable progress in the modernization of railways, electrification schemes, expansion of maritime trade, and industrialization. However, 40% of the working population was still engaged in agriculture.

During Salazar's rule, tourism in Portugal saw significant growth. In the context of World War II, Portugal maintained a stance of neutrality and entered into a non-aggression pact with Spain. In 1943, Portugal reaffirmed its long-standing alliance with Britain, allowing the British to use the Azores Islands as military bases. After the war, Portugal joined NATO in 1949, although its decision was not directly linked to its wartime neutrality or stance against opposition groups. Unlike other colonial powers that were rapidly decolonizing, Salazar was determined to maintain Portugal's overseas territories. He remained in power until he was incapacitated by a stroke in 1968 and died in 1970.

Under the Estado Novo's economic policy of corporatism, a few powerful conglomerates gained control over large segments of Portugal's economy. Prominent among these were conglomerates established by the Manuel, Champalimaud, and dos Santos families, who became particularly influential. One of the most significant conglomerates was Companhia União Fabril (CUF), which had a diverse portfolio, including sectors such as electrical and naval engineering, agrochemicals, cement, beverages, and textiles. CUF had an extensive presence across Portugal with various projects, branches, and plants.

By the early 1970s, Portugal also had many medium-sized companies specializing in textiles, porcelain, ceramics, crystal, glass, wood, and canned fish. In rural areas, families primarily engaged in forestry and agriculture. In addition, Portugal's overseas colonies served as significant sources for resource extraction, providing metals, minerals, timber, cotton, coffee, and other goods.

After Salazar's death, Marcello Caetano succeeded him as prime minister and ruled Portugal as a dictator. Initially, Caetano relaxed some of Salazar's repressive policies, particularly those targeting political opposition and the media, and increased the education budget. However, his early liberal reforms gradually diminished. The military became increasingly dissatisfied with his policies in Portugal's African colonies. In 1972, Caetano granted greater autonomy to Mozambique and Angola but continued Salazar's militaristic approach to suppress local insurgencies. These military efforts drained over 40% of Portugal's national budget. In 1974, a military coup ousted Caetano's government. Following the coup, General António de Spínola became the President of Portugal, while

Adelino da Palma Carlos was appointed Prime Minister, leading a provisional government.

General Spínola came into office with promises to the Portuguese people. He promised to restore constitutional democracy and to hold elections within a year. He also announced a policy of "decolonization"—the withdrawal of Portuguese troops from Africa and the early grant of independence to the colonies. General Gomez, a key military figure, stepped into leadership during a turbulent time in the country's history. Over the preceding two years, the political landscape had been fraught with instability as communist factions attempted to seize governmental control. In the wake of this chaos, Spínola resigned in late 1974, paving the way for General Gomez to take the reins. Meanwhile, the independence movements that had started in Portuguese African colonies during Salazar's time were gaining more ground. The earlier regimes had responded by giving more and more of Portugal's budget to suppressing those uprisings. The country became increasingly isolated, facing armed embargoes, international sanctions, and internal strife.

When General Gomez assumed leadership, the military was stretched thin, with no clear political resolution for the ongoing issues. Guerrilla casualties were rising, and Portugal faced mounting criticism from the international community. Incidents like the Wiriyamu Massacre, in which Portuguese troops attacked the Mozambican village of Wiriyamu, further eroded the country's global standing and weakened its diplomatic leverage. Domestically, the war was deeply unpopular, contributing to a growing polarization within the country. In protest, thousands of anti-war activists and left-leaning students dodged compulsory enlistment by fleeing the country. Most sought refuge in France, while some went to the United States.

During the era of Portugal's authoritarian Estado Novo regime, two generations of right-wing militants, partly influenced by the rise of neo-fascism in Europe, lent their support to the government. At the same time, Portugal was deeply affected by ongoing colonial wars in Africa. This backdrop of conflict and discontent motivated the Armed Forces Movement (MFA) to insti- gate the Carnation Revolution in 1974, aiming to free the country from authoritarian rule and end colonial wars. Following the revolution, the transitional govern- ment enacted new military laws to reduce the alloca- tion of national resources to the military and restructure it. Many young graduates were unhappy with being drafted into service in the colonial territo- ries as part of these military reforms.

When General Gomez assumed the presidency, he decided to finalize the decolonization process in Africa. As a result, Cape Verde, Angola, Guinea-Bissau, and Mozambique gained independence in 1974. After these events, Portugal retained only a few overseas territories: Madeira and the Azores in the Atlantic and Macau in China.

10

THE CARNATION REVOLUTION, THE THIRD REPUBLIC, AND MODERN-DAY PORTUGAL (1975–2022 AD)

The end of the First Republic in Portugal occurred in 1926, giving way to a period of military dictatorship. The Estado Novo, or "New State," was officially established in 1933 by António de Oliveira Salazar, marking the definitive end of the unstable Second Republic and ushering in an authoritarian regime. Salazar stepped down due to ill health in 1968, and Marcelo Caetano succeeded him. By the time Caetano was in office, the country was ripe for political change. This pent-up desire for reform led to the Carnation Revolution of 1974, where protestors symbolically placed carnations in the barrels of soldiers' rifles as a sign of peace. This revolution marked the end of the Estado Novo and the beginning of the Third Republic. The country erupted in celebrations that nearly five decades of dictatorship had finally concluded. Politicians like Mário Soares and Álvaro Cunhal, who had been in exile, returned to Portugal and became iconic figures in the newly restored democracy.

Today, the revolution is celebrated on the 25th of April. It was led by left-leaning military officers whose goal was to overthrow the Estado Novo. It succeeded in 1974 in Lisbon, creating significant changes in the country's economic, demographic, social, and political spheres and triggering the decolonization of Portugal's overseas colonies. The revolution spurred the country's transition into a democracy, which it remains to this day.

In 1974, Portugal was at a crossroads concerning its future direction. Marcelo Caetano was in power, and a group of military officers who disagreed with him formed the Armed Forces Movement (MFA). These officers were sympathetic to the ideas of General António de Spínola, who had articulated his vision for the country's future. The MFA initiated what began as a military coup, which was soon bolstered by a widespread civil resistance campaign. Within the Portuguese army, the MFA received support from other officers who shared pro-Spínola sentiments and favored military and democratic reforms. This collective effort culminated in the Carnation Revolution, setting the stage for the end of the Estado Novo regime and the beginning of democratic governance in Portugal.

In 1974, two distinct signals were used to initiate the coup that led to the Carnation Revolution. The first signal was the airing of Paulo de Carvalho's entry in that year's Eurovision Song Contest, which served as a prearranged cue for the rebel soldiers and captains to commence their actions. The second signal came at 12:20 a.m. when Radio Renascença broadcast a song by Zeca Afonso, a prominent political folk musician whose work had been banned from the station at that time. These two signals served as coordinated triggers for the rebels to begin taking control of key strategic locations across the country.

The fall of Marcelo Caetano's government took approximately six hours. Although the captains involved in the MFA repeatedly urged civilians to stay home for their safety, thousands defied the warnings. They took to the streets in support of the military insurgents. Carnations, sourced from the city's flower market where people had gathered, became the symbolic flower of the revolution. Caetano sought refuge in a building in Lisbon, but members of the MFA quickly surrounded it. Ultimately, he was forced to relinquish power to General António de Spínola. After stepping down, Caetano fled to Brazil, where he lived for the remainder of his life.

While there were no large-scale demonstrations preceding the coup, the spontaneous involvement of civilians transformed it into a popular revolution led by soldiers, officers, peasants, and workers. The revolution earned its "Carnation" moniker because it was remarkably nonviolent, with virtually no shots fired. A restaurant worker named Celeste Caeiro is credited with handing out carnations to soldiers, a gesture that the public emulated by placing the flowers on gun barrels during subsequent demonstrations. Although there were later attempts to steer the revolution in a more radical direction, these efforts were effectively quelled by the Socialist Party.

The coup in Portugal was remarkably peaceful, although government forces shot four civilians. The MFA subsequently brought those responsible to justice. After the coup, the National Salvation Junta assumed control of the government, leading Portugal into a period commonly referred to as the "Ongoing Revolutionary Process." In the beginning, conservative elements led by General António de Spínola clashed with the MFA, prompting Spínola to appoint key MFA figures to senior positions in an attempt to ease tensions. A counter-coup attempt by right-wing officers failed, resulting in Spínola's resignation and departure from office. Internal divisions within the MFA eventually led to its disbandment. The country remained politically unstable until the end of 1975, with continuous tensions between leftist-communist and liberal-democratic factions. The first free elections were held, leading to the drafting of a new constitution to replace the one from 1933. Mário Soares assumed office after winning the 1976 election.

The revolution started negotiations with independent movements in Africa, and in 1974, Portuguese troops withdrew from Guinea. Guinea went on to become a member state of the United Nations. The other African countries followed suit in 1975. The process of decolonization led to a large-scale departure of Portuguese citizens from former territories, particularly from Mozambique and Angola. This resulted in the displacement of more than one million Portuguese refugees.

The Portuguese 1976 constitution made life better in many ways. It guaranteed that all religions have a right to practice. Non-Catholic groups finally gained legal recognition, allowing them the right to assemble. Despite this, the Catholic Church continued efforts to restrict the activities of other missionary groups.

Before the revolution, Portugal experienced strong annual GDP growth and increased industrial production, consumption, and gross fixed capital formation. However, the economy slowed significantly during the revolutionary period. The country's entry into the European Economic Community (EEC) served as a primary driver for economic improvement at that time. Although Portugal never regained its pre-revolution growth rates, it's important to note that the country was underdeveloped during the revolution, with inefficient agricultural practices, inadequate infrastructure, and some of Europe's lowest education and health indicators.

Before the revolution, Portugal did experience some periods of economic and social progress. After enduring a lengthy phase of economic decline, the country saw a modest recovery until 1950. From then onward, Portugal entered a growth phase until 1980, aligning it with other growing economies in Western Europe. Despite this, Portugal remained one of the poorest countries in the region during this period.

Under the Estado Novo regime, Portugal's economic growth created opportunities for closer integration with the more developed economies of Western Europe. Through avenues like trade, foreign investment, tourism, and emigration, both companies and individuals in Portugal began to change their consumption and production habits. This led to a more complex and diversified economy, which in turn presented new organizational and technical challenges.

In 1972, a sovereign wealth fund was established to finance Portugal's colonial wars in Africa, as the financial strain of the conflict became increasingly difficult for the government to manage. To offset these costs, laws were enacted to curtail military expenses and increase the officer corps by recruiting from military academies. Concurrently, land reforms were implemented. According to government estimates, nearly 2.2 million acres of agricultural land were confiscated as part of these reforms, with 32% of these seizures later deemed illegal. In 1976, the government committed to returning land that had been illegally appropriated, and the restoration process began in 1978.

In the early 1960s, Portugal's per-capita GDP was 38% of the EEC average. By the time Salazar stepped down from power, this figure had increased to 48%. It rose to 56.4% by 1973 but dropped to 52.3% in 1975. Several factors contributed to this economic decline, including a recession in Europe, the economic policies implemented during the revolutionary period, oil shocks, and the influx of Portuguese refugees returning from Africa. Economic growth resumed in 1985, and by

1991, Portugal's per-capita GDP slightly surpassed the EEC average.

In 2011, a Portuguese tabloid newspaper reported economic mismanagement from 1975 to 2010, implicating a succession of governments in fostering investment bubbles, overspending in public-private partnerships, and accumulating public debt. Prime Minister Jose Socrates, who took office in 2005 following a landslide victory for the Socialist Party, could not mitigate these long-term issues. By 2011, Portugal teetered on the brink of bankruptcy and sought assistance from the European Union and the IMF.

Antonio Guterres had initially ushered in this era of political turnover when he became Prime Minister in 1995, serving until his resignation in 2001 following electoral setbacks. His exit paved the way for Jose Manuel Barroso, who stepped down in 2004 to become President of the European Commission. Pedro Santana Lopes briefly assumed the role before the Socialist Party, under Jose Socrates, regained power in 2005. Socrates navigated through reelection in 2009, albeit with a diminished majority, forcing him to lead a minority government.

During this politically fluid period, Portugal underwent significant changes. It adopted the euro in 2002 and hosted the Euro 2004 soccer championship, losing the final to Greece but gaining an opportunity to showcase its hosting capabilities. Amidst these societal shifts, a presidential election was held in 2006 to find a successor for Jorge Sampaio. Anibal Cavaco Silva of the Social Democratic Party emerged victorious, with a voter turnout of 62.60%.

Starting in 2008, Portugal felt the severe impact of the European debt crisis, exacerbated by years of excessive borrowing. The country's unsustainable debt levels brought the economy close to collapse, necessitating significant structural reforms to cut public sector spending and increase taxes. Portugal became the third country to seek financial assistance from the European Union and the IMF, following Ireland and Greece. In 2015, Prime Minister Pedro Passos Coelho secured a narrow electoral victory, forming a new minority government. However, this government lasted only eleven days, setting a record for Portugal's shortest national government. As of 2021, Marcelo Rebelo de Sousa served as the President of Portugal, having been reelected with 60.7% of the vote in the first round.

In the sweeping tapestry of its history, Portugal has proven itself a nation of resilience and reinvention. From its Age of Discovery to its peaceful transition to democracy, Portugal's past is a testament to its enduring spirit and adaptability. As the country enters the 21st century, it is buoyed by a rich cultural heritage and a history of overcoming adversity. Yet, Portugal's story is far from over. Its willingness to adapt and innovate positions it well for the challenges and opportunities of a rapidly changing world. With its roots firmly in its storied past and its gaze fixed on a promising future, Portugal is poised to continue making impactful contributions to the global stage.

As we close this chapter, remember that the history recounted here is merely a prologue to a future still unfolding. And in that future, Portugal stands ready to write yet another inspiring chapter, reflective not just of a single nation but of the enduring human spirit.

Thank you for journeying through Portugal's intricate and fascinating history with *A Brief History of Portugal: Blazing the Trail of a Voyage-Shaped Nation*. Your engagement as a reader enriches the narrative and helps to keep these important stories alive. If you've found value in these pages, I kindly ask that you consider leaving a review. Your insights help potential readers make an informed choice and provide invaluable feedback for future works. Once again, thank you for your engagement; it has been a privilege to share Portugal's rich history with you.

OTHER BOOKS BY DOMINIC HAYNES

(AVAILABLE ON AMAZON & AUDIBLE)

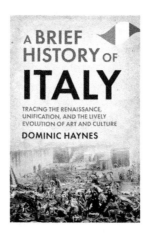

A Brief History of Italy: Tracing the Renaissance,
Unification, and the Lively Evolution of Art and Culture

A Brief History of Central Banking: How the Quest for
Financial Stability Led to Unconventional Monetary
Practices

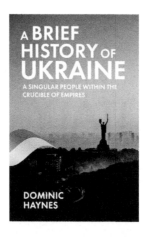

A Brief History of Ukraine: A Singular People Within the
Crucible of Empires

REFERENCES

Amerigo Vespucci. (2023, September 8). In *Encyclopedia Britannica*. https://www.britannica.com/biography/Amerigo-Vespucci

Barton, S., & Portass, R. (Eds.). (2020). *Beyond the Reconquista: New Directions in the History of Medieval Iberia (711–1085)*. BRILL.

Birmingham, D. (2018). *A Concise History of Portugal*. Cambridge University Press.

Braganca, house of. (n.d.). In Encyclopedia.com. https://www.encyclopedia.com/humanities/encyclopedias-almanacs-transcripts-and-maps/Braganca-house

C. T. (2015, November 27). The Iberians. *Portugal Online*. https://portugalonline.com/portugal/information/history/iberians

Calógeras, J. P. (1939). *A History of Brazil*. A UNC Press Enduring Edition.

Charles River Editors. (2018). *The Reconquista: The History and Legacy of the Conflicts between the Moors and Christians on the Iberian Peninsula*.

Conquest of Ceuta. (n.d.). In *StudySmarter UK*. Retrieved September 13, 2023, from https://www.studysmarter.co.uk/explanations/history/modern-world-history/conquest-of-ceuta/

Curley, W. J. (1973). *Monarchs-in-waiting*. Dodd, Mead.

Davidson, L. C. (2022). *Catherine of Braganca, Infanta of Portugal, & Queen-consort of England*. Legare Street Press.

Estado Novo. (2023, July 23). In *Encyclopedia Britannica*. https://www.britannica.com/topic/Estado-Novo-Portuguese-history

Exploring the Past in Portugal. (2021, May 8). *Archaeology Travel*. https://archaeology-travel.com/destinations/europe/portugal/

First Punic War. (2023, August 25). In *Encyclopedia Britannica*. https://www.britannica.com/event/First-Punic-War

Disney, A. R. (2012, June 5). Gharb Al-Andalus. In *Cambridge Core*. https://www.cambridge.org/core/books/abs/history-of-portugal-

and-the-portuguese-empire/gharb-alandalus/
48DA6BCEBF81D350F54BF0F358633FAA

Gharb al–andalus. (2022, July 26). *PORTICO magazine by Vanguard Properties.* https://www.portico-magazine.com/articles/gharb-al-andalus

History of Portugal (1640–1777). (2022, October 19). In *Wikipedia.* https://en.wikipedia.org/wiki/History_of_Portugal_(1640%E2%80%931777)

Iberian Union. (n.d.). In DBpedia. https://dbpedia.org/page/Iberian_Union

Key Events in Portuguese History. (2011, August 26). *ThoughtCo.* https://www.thoughtco.com/events-in-portuguese-history-1221724

Lillios, K. T. (1995). *The Origins of Complex Societies in Late Prehistoric Iberia.* International Monographs in Prehistory.

Michie, A. A. (1952). *The Crown and the People.* Secker & Warburg.

Monteiro, N. G. (n.d.). Aristocratic succession in Portugal (From the sixteenth to the nineteenth centuries). *OpenEdition Books.* https://books.openedition.org/etnograficapress/1359?lang=en

Napoleon I - Downfall and abdication. (2023, July 25). In *Encyclopedia Britannica.* https://www.britannica.com/biography/Napoleon-I/Downfall-and-abdication

Nicolle, D. (1988). *El CID and the Reconquista 1050–1492.* Osprey Publishing.

Osório, J. (1752). *The history of the Portuguese, during the reign of Emmanuel.* A. Millar, London.

Philip III. (n.d.). In *Encyclopedia Britannica.* Retrieved September 13, 2023, from https://www.britannica.com/biography/Philip-III-king-of-Spain-and-Portugal

Philip of Spain. (1997, August 10). *The New York Times Web Archive.* https://archive.nytimes.com/www.nytimes.com/books/first/k/kamen-philip.html

Portugal - Iberian Union. (n.d.). *Country Studies.* Retrieved September 13, 2023, from https://countrystudies.us/portugal/29.htm

The Portuguese Revolution of 5 October 1910. (2022, September 22).

Portugal.com. https://www.portugal.com/history-and-culture/the-portuguese-revolution-of-1910/

Portuguese Succession Crisis. (2022, December 8). *Wikiwand.* https://www.wikiwand.com/en/1580_Portuguese_succession_crisis

Prehistoric Rock Art Sites in the CoA Valley and Siega Verde, Portugal and Spain. (n.d.). *Google Arts & Culture.* https://artsandculture.google.com/story/prehistoric-rock-art-sites-in-the-c%C3%B4a-valley-and-siega-verde-portugal-and-spain-unesco/_wUR1c4F5qaxIQ?hl=en

Reconquista: How the Christian Kingdoms took Spain from the Moors. (2022, January 5). *TheCollector.* https://www.thecollector.com/reconquista-christian-reconquest-of-spain/

Wintle, M. (2015). *Europe in the Eighteenth Century.* Macmillan.

Zimbalist, A. (2004). *Sport and Development in Portugal.* Routledge.

Printed in Great Britain
by Amazon